NEW YORK
PENNSYLVANIA
NEW JERSEY
50 HIKES
WITH KIDS

NEW YORK
PENNSYLVANIA
NEW JERSEY
50 HIKES
WITH KIDS

WENDY GORTON

Timber Press · Portland, Oregon

Published in 2022 by Timber Press, Inc.
The Haseltine Building
133 S.W. Second Avenue, Suite 450
Portland, Oregon 97204-3527
timberpress.com

Printed in China on paper from responsible sources

Series design by Hillary Caudle; layout by Sarah Crumb
Cover design and illustration by Always With Honor
Inside cover map by David Deis

ISBN 978-1-64326-002-0

A catalog record for this book is available from the Library of Congress.

For my baby girl,
who was with me for every step of this journey;
I can't wait to show you more!

CONTENTS

PREFACE

"Let's hike the Appalachian Trail!" One day, your little adventurers might suggest this, and hopefully you'll be able to join them on a section of that amazing 2,190-mile trail that runs through parts of New York, Pennsylvania, and New Jersey, among other states. Aside from the Appalachian Trail, however, this part of the mid-Atlantic region offers a remarkable diversity of terrain and adventure that is sure to satisfy both you and your young explorers.

This guide aims to provide kids of all ages a curated selection of some of the most varied and interesting destinations in these three states, while reassuring and preparing busy adults so that they know what to expect from any given trail, the features they will see when they arrive, and the logistics that can make or break an outdoor excursion with kids. I hope you get a sense of the love steeped in these pages—love for the outdoors, love for adventure, love for planning and preparation, and love for family and community. My family members were my coadventurers on every hike, tackling bathroom mishaps, downed trees, and even multiple hikes a day to test and compare, because choosing which adventures to include was no easy task. There are a lot of kid-friendly hikes in the region, but I developed a firm kid filter, one that includes awesome features, simple driving, and turnkey instructions on the trail so you're not second-guessing yourselves. My filter also ensures honest-to-goodness dirt on the bottom of your shoes and no long-winded interpretive installations. It's all aimed at giving you a more adventurous hiking experience rather than a sterile stroll.

Many of us have seen the copious amounts of research about the benefits of getting kids outdoors more and interacting with the world in an open-ended way. As you romp with your own crew through the outdoors, just keep in mind that while the scavenger hunt items called out on each

∧ **Autumn is often a good time for an adventure—changing leaves and fewer crowds**

hike might add excitement or teachable moments, finding them all should not be the main goal of your outing. I wrote this guide to help you get outside, spend time with your family, and have fun.

In 2006, smack in the middle of my second year of teaching fourth graders, I became a PolarTREC GoNorth! teacher explorer. I packed up with a top-notch, experienced adventure crew, and we set out to spend two weeks dog sledding, interviewing locals about climate change, and collecting snowpack data. My number-one goal was to interpret the experience for my students back in my classroom and students around the world who wanted to feel like they were part of a real-life adventure. Every night, our dogs rushed us through the snow to the next research hut in the middle of Finland. Once inside, we peeled off our layers, cooked dinner from our meal rations, used our maps to plan the next day, and got a good night's sleep.

Then as now, I studied each day's route with the eyes of a child—finding the nooks that delighted me, asking myself big questions, documenting things that interested me but that I couldn't identify on the spot, and researching answers. A decade and a half later, I'm thrilled to be creating mini adventures for families, helping you become intrepid adventurers too.

The driving question behind this book is: how can we design experiences that inspire wonder in our children? That's also a question I encourage you to keep in mind as you use this book. If we can provide a fun environment and the initial sparks of curiosity, we can—as educators, caregivers, aunties and uncles, grandparents, and parents—help children discover and explore the world around them, creating a generation of resilient, curious kids who appreciate natural beauty even from a young age. This book tries to give adults some tools to help ignite questions on the trail, to teach kids that it's great to stop and look at things instead of just rushing from point A to point B, and to begin to introduce a broader understanding of just how many unique places surround us in this part of the mid-Atlantic. By simply venturing out and interacting with kids along the trail, we are building their skills in questioning things they see around them—everywhere—and encouraging them to look for answers.

Peter Gray, a Boston College research professor and expert on children's play, encourages parents to include other kids on adventures: "When you go on a hike or a trip, think about inviting other families or joining group hikes. Kids need other kids. This frees you, the adult, as well as your child, so you can interact with other adults. They can go ahead safely on the trail, and you don't have to go and amuse them because they are learning and playing with their peers. Don't try to cover too much ground—stop and let them play wherever they are."

Kids lead more structured lives today than ever before. I think you'll be pleasantly surprised when you see how much they enjoy simply being set loose in wide-open spaces. I hope this guide will help you foster curiosity and a love of nature in the kids in your life and that it helps to raise our next generation of naturalists by putting the guidebook in their hands. Many of the adventures in this book provide a taste of treks kids may embark on

∧ The northern mid-Atlantic states are full of beautiful bodies of water, from waterfalls to rivers and lakes

as college students or adults—imagine them tackling a list like the one at 4000footers.com. There is a proud tradition of marking trail maps with red pen each time you complete a hike. I encourage you to grab your own pen and mark your achievements in guidebooks and maps as your family grows up. Experiencing the wonders all around us creates lifelong habits of seeking out adventure, appreciating the gifts nature gives us every day, and caring about keeping our natural resources clean, beautiful, and accessible for future generations. All the scaffolds you'll need to plan even more of your own adventures are here.

CHOOSING YOUR ADVENTURE

This guide is designed to help children become coadventurers with you across the diverse northern mid-Atlantic landscape, so build excitement by involving them in the planning process from the beginning. Let them flip through and mark the hikes they'd like to tackle in the future. Ask them what features they love when they're outside. How hard do they feel like working today for their adventure? How long do they want to hike? The tables in this chapter can help you choose. For maximum success with younger kids, no hike is over 5 miles long or gains more than 1,000 feet—perfectly attainable for most little legs. This means that there can be plenty of time for exploration, rest stops, snacks, and just taking in the sights and sounds around you.

ADVENTURES IN NEW YORK

ADVENTURE	NEAREST CITY	LENGTH (MILES)	DIFFICULTY & ELEVATION (FEET)	HIGHLIGHTS
1 Shadmoor State Park PAGE 58	Montauk	1.3	Easy 45'	Beach, history, geology
2 Harriman State Park PAGE 62	Harriman	3.3	Challenging 243'	Mine, swamp, mountain laurel
3 Constitution Marsh PAGE 66	Cold Spring	2.5	Moderate 164'	Birdwatching, boardwalk
4 Dover Stone Church PAGE 70	Dover Plains	1	Easy 123'	Waterfalls, cave, river
5 Lake Minnewaska PAGE 74	New Paltz	2.3	Moderate 140'	Lake, geology, history
6 Black Creek Preserve PAGE 78	Esopus	2.1	Moderate 187'	Suspension bridge, creek, views
7 Catskill Mountain House PAGE 82	Palenville	1.7	Moderate 271'	History, views, geology
8 Indian Ladder Trail PAGE 86	New Salem/ Albany	1	Moderate 160'	History, ladders, geology
9 Shelving Rock PAGE 90	Lake George	3.1	Challenging 595'	Views, history
10 Cobble Hill PAGE 94	Lake Placid	2.3	Moderate 495'	Rope, views, geology

ADVENTURE	NEAREST CITY	LENGTH (MILES)	DIFFICULTY & ELEVATION (FEET)	HIGHLIGHTS
11 **Mount Arab Fire Tower** PAGE 98	Piercefield	2.1	Challenging 727'	Fire tower, views
12 **Stone Valley** PAGE 102	Colton/ Potsdam	1.8	Moderate 131'	River, waterfalls, history
13 **Bald Mountain Fire Tower** PAGE 106	Old Forge	2	Moderate 376'	Fire tower, geology
14 **Beaver Lake** PAGE 110	Baldwinsville	2.8	Easy 60'	Boardwalk, marsh, lake
15 **Auburn Trail** PAGE 114	Pittsford	1.4	Easy 35'	Birds, history
16 **Niagara Whirlpool** PAGE 118	Niagara	2.4	Moderate 285'	River, geology
17 **Eternal Flame Falls** PAGE 122	Orchard Park/ Buffalo	1.2	Moderate 140'	Natural gas flame, creek, geology
18 **Watkins Glen** PAGE 126	Watkins Glen/ Seneca Lake	2.3	Moderate 433'	Waterfalls, stone stairs
19 **Taughannock Falls** PAGE 130	Ithaca	2	Easy 75'	Waterfall, river

ADVENTURES IN PENNSYLVANIA

ADVENTURE	NEAREST CITY	LENGTH (MILES)	DIFFICULTY & ELEVATION (FEET)	HIGHLIGHTS
20 **Governor Dick Observation Tower** PAGE 136	Harrisburg	1	Moderate 318'	Cool tower, benches, fun gates to pass through
21 **P. Joseph Raab Park** PAGE 140	York	2.4	Moderate 85'	Historical mines, cool quartz, creek
22 **Pole Steeple** PAGE 144	Harrisburg	1.9	Challenging 539'	Viewpoint, awesome rocks, the chance to step on the famous AT
23 **Trough Creek** PAGE 148	James Creek	1	Easy 90'	Suspension bridge, walls, river, geology
24 **Allegheny Portage Railroad** PAGE 152	Johnstown	4.4	Challenging 20'	Tunnel, history
25 **Ohiopyle Slides** PAGE 156	Ohiopyle	2.8	Challenging 196'	River
26 **Roaring Run** PAGE 160	Apollo	2	Moderate 194'	Suspension bridge, history
27 **Mineral Springs** PAGE 164	Hookstown	1.2	Moderate 209'	Ruins, waterfall, springs
28 **Tamarack Trail** PAGE 168	Jamestown	1.3	Easy 22'	Dams

ADVENTURE	NEAREST CITY	LENGTH (MILES)	DIFFICULTY & ELEVATION (FEET)	HIGHLIGHTS
29 **Presque Isle State Park** PAGE 172	Erie	2.5	Easy 6'	Birdwatching, beach, history
30 **Rimrock Trail** PAGE 176	Bradford	3.3	Challenging 600'	Views, geology, beach
31 **Kinzua Bridge** PAGE 180	Jewett	1.5	Moderate 292'	Ruins, views, history
32 **Otter Point** PAGE 184	Ansonia	1	Moderate 238'	Views, history
33 **Double Run** PAGE 188	Laporte	2	Moderate 300'	Falls, birdwatching
34 **Ricketts Glen** PAGE 192	Fairmount Township	3.3	Challenging 715'	Falls, geology
35 **Ringing Rocks** PAGE 196	Upper Black Eddy	1.3	Easy 133'	Waterfall and musical rocks
36 **Dingmans Falls** PAGE 200	Dingmans Ferry	1.4	Easy 249'	Falls, boardwalk, staircase
37 **Buttermilk and Luke's Falls** PAGE 204	Weatherly	1.2	Easy 22'	Two falls

ADVENTURES IN
NEW JERSEY

ADVENTURE	NEAREST CITY	LENGTH (MILES)	DIFFICULTY & ELEVATION (FEET)	HIGHLIGHTS
38 Palisades Interstate Park PAGE 210	Alpine	1.5	Moderate 112'	Birdwatching
39 South Mountain Reservation PAGE 214	Millburn	1	Easy 35'	Unique fairy houses, dam
40 Pyramid Mountain PAGE 218	Boonton	3	Challenging 296'	View, geology
41 Van Slyke Castle PAGE 222	Wanaque	2.2	Moderate 172'	Historical ruins
42 Pochuck Suspension Bridge PAGE 226	Vernon Township	1.6	Easy 29'	Boardwalk, suspension bridge
43 Tillman's Ravine PAGE 230	Branchville	1.6	Moderate 368'	History, creek, water feature

ADVENTURE	NEAREST CITY	LENGTH (MILES)	DIFFICULTY & ELEVATION (FEET)	HIGHLIGHTS
44 Pahaquarry *PAGE 234*	Hardwick Township	0.5	Easy 98'	Copper mines, history, falls
45 Black River *PAGE 238*	Chester Township	3.7	Moderate 118'	River, historical ruins
46 Goat Hill Overlook *PAGE 242*	Lambertville	1	Easy 162'	History, view
47 Swinging Bridge *PAGE 246*	Princeton	2.4	Easy 76'	Swinging bridge, history, canal
48 Cattus Island *PAGE 250*	Toms River	2.3	Easy 7'	Birdwatching, ocean views
49 Batsto Village *PAGE 254*	Hammonton	1.5	Easy 32'	History, lake
50 Cape May *PAGE 258*	Cape May	1.9	Easy 8'	Lighthouse, beach, birdwatching, history

∧ The historic ruins of Van Slyke Castle can be found during your New Jersey adventures

ADVENTURES BY FEATURE

Can you remember the first cave you explored? The first waterfall that misted your face? Each of these adventures includes a destination or item of particular interest to motivate young legs and reward hard work. Encourage kids, as coadventurers, to talk about which types of natural features tickle them the most and why.

FEATURE	ADVENTURE
Lakes	(2) Lake Skannatati at Harriman State Park
	(5) Lake Minnewaska
	(9) Lake George at Shelving Rock
	(10) Mirror and Echo Lakes at Cobble Hill
	(14) Beaver Lake
	(22) Laurel Lake at Pole Steeple
	(28) Reservoir at Tamarack Trail
	(30) Allegheny Reservoir at Rimrock Trail
	(45) Kay Pond at Black River
	(49) Batsto Lake at Batsto Village
Waterfalls	(4) Cave Falls at Dover Stone Church
	(12) Stone Valley waterfalls
	(17) Eternal Flame Falls
	(18) Watkins Glen
	(19) Taughannock Falls
	(23) Rainbow Falls at Trough Creek
	(25) Cascades Waterfall at Ohiopyle Slides
	(27) Mineral Springs
	(32) Falls at Otter Point
	(33) Cottonwood Falls at Double Run
	(34) Ricketts Glen
	(35) High Falls at Ringing Rocks
	(36) Dingmans Falls
	(37) Buttermilk and Luke's Falls
	(44) Falls at Pahaquarry

FEATURE	ADVENTURE
History	① World War II artifacts at Shadmoor State Park
	② Pine Swamp Mine at Harriman State Park
	④ Dover Stone Church
	⑤ Old carriage roads at Lake Minnewaska
	⑦ Catskill Mountain House
	⑧ Indian Ladder Trail
	⑨ Carriage trail to Shelving Rock
	⑪ Mount Arab Fire Tower
	⑬ Bald Mountain Fire Tower
	⑮ Old railroad on the Auburn Trail
	⑱ CCC bridges at Watkins Glen
	⑳ Governor Dick Observation Tower
	㉑ Mine at P. Joseph Raab Park
	㉔ Allegheny Portage Railroad
	㉖ Biddle Rock Furnace at Jackson Falls
	㉗ Ruins at Mineral Springs
	㉙ Sidewalk Trail at Presque Isle
	㊴ Dam at South Mountain Reservation
	㊶ Van Slyke Castle
	㊷ Pochuck Suspension Bridge and Boardwalk
	㊺ Kay's Cottage at Black River
	㊻ Goat Hill Overlook
	㊾ Batsto Village
	㊿ Lighthouse and World War II structures at Cape May

FEATURE	ADVENTURE
Flora	**1** Shadbush at Shadmoor State Park
	2 Early summer mountain laurel at Harriman State Park
	6 Vernal pools at Black Creek Preserve
	10 Hobblebush at Cobble Hill
	14 Pitcher plant at Beaver Lake
	22 Pitch pine at Pole Steeple
	25 Early summer rhododendron at Ohiopyle Slides
	27 Spring trillium at Mineral Springs
Fauna	**3** Birdwatch at Constitution Marsh
	5 Fall Hawkwatch at Lake Minnewaska
	6 Vernal pools at Black Creek Preserve
	8 Red eft newts at Indian Ladder Trail
	14 Turtles, beavers, and birds at Beaver Lake
	15 Birdwatch on the Auburn Trail
	21 Bats at P. Joseph Raab Park
	38 Hawkwatch at Palisades Interstate Park
	42 Deer at Pochuck Suspension Bridge
	48 Birdwatch on Cattus Island
	50 Birdwatch at Cape May

FEATURE	ADVENTURE
Geology	① Hoodoo formations at Shadmoor State Park
	④ Cave at Dover Stone Church
	⑤ Quartz at Lake Minnewaska
	⑦ Boulder Rock near Catskill Mountain House
	⑧ Gorge on Indian Ladder Trail
	⑫ Potholes at Stone Valley
	⑬ Bald Mountain
	⑯ Rocks at Niagara Whirlpool
	⑰ Eternal Flame
	㉒ Quartzite at Pole Steeple
	㉓ Balanced Rock in Trough Creek
	㉕ Ohiopyle Slides
	㉗ Mineral Springs
	㉚ Overlook on Rimrock Trail
	㉟ Ringing Rocks
	㊵ Tripod Rock on Pyramid Mountain
	㊸ Teacup at Tillman's Ravine
Caves	② Caves and Mines at Harriman State Park
	㉑ Mines at P. Joseph Raab Park
	㊹ Copper Mines at Pahaquarry
Summits, peaks, views	⑦ View at Catskill Mountain House
	⑨ Summit at Shelving Rock
	⑩ Cobble Hill
	⑪ Mount Arab Fire Tower
	⑬ Bald Mountain Fire Tower
	⑳ Governor Dick Observation Tower
	㉒ Pole Steeple
	㉜ Otter Point
	㊳ Viewpoint at Palisades Interstate Park
	㊻ Goat Hill Overlook

FEATURE	ADVENTURE
River and creek exploration	(4) Stone Church Brook at Dover Stone Church
	(6) Hudson River at Black Creek Preserve
	(12) Raquette River at Stone Valley
	(16) Niagara Whirlpool
	(23) Abbott Run at Trough Creek
	(25) Meadow Run at Ohiopyle Slides
	(33) Double Run
	(34) Ricketts Glen
	(43) Tillman Brook at Tillman's Ravine
	(45) Black River
	(47) Swinging Bridge
Beach fun	(1) Ocean beach at Shadmoor State Park
	(48) Mosquito Cove at Cattus Island
	(50) Ocean beach at Cape May
Campground by trailhead	(1) Shadmoor State Park
	(2) Harriman State Park
	(5) Lake Minnewaska
	(7) Catskill Mountain House
	(9) Shelving Rock
	(11) Mount Arab
	(18) Watkins Glen
	(22) Pole Steeple
	(25) Ohiopyle Slides
	(27) Mineral Springs
	(36) Dingmans Falls
	(43) Tillman's Ravine

∧ The trail to Mount Arab
Fire Tower in fall

ADVENTURES BY SEASON

Many trails are available year-round for your adventuring pleasure, yet some really sing during particular moments of the year. Prepare your family to be ready for any season. Spring is often great for wildflower blooms or trails with waterfalls at maximum flow, but for some trails it's mud season—check conditions beforehand (and make sure the trail isn't closed), wear appropriate footwear, and consider using a hiking stick or trekking poles. Summer allows the best access to more exposed, rocky trails that might be slippery or treacherous during winter, along with special, higher-elevation wildflowers, but the season also comes with copious flies and ticks—bring repellent and always do full-body checks afterward. In fall, many trails erupt with color and mushrooms, but some trails go near areas that allow hunting—always read the posted signs and consider carrying orange shirts and hats in your adventure bag. Winter can be a great time to escape crowds, especially if you bring your snowshoes or ice tracks. Keep in mind that any prime season (summer for hikes near swimming areas or fall for the most leafalicious hikes) means you might encounter crowds, so consider visiting early or late in the day, or try exploring during an off-season. Allow your kids to understand the seasons by returning to a favorite hike throughout the year and asking them what's changed since their last visit.

PEAK SEASON	ADVENTURE	
Winter	⑥ Black Creek Preserve	㉗ Mineral Springs
	⑪ Mount Arab	㉚ Rimrock Trail
	⑫ Stone Valley	㊳ Palisades Interstate Park
	⑬ Bald Mountain Fire Tower	㊻ Goat Hill Overlook
Spring	⑥ Black Creek Preserve	⑲ Taughannock Falls
	⑩ Cobble Hill	⑳ Governor Dick
	⑫ Stone Valley	Observation Tower
	⑭ Beaver Lake	㉓ Trough Creek
	⑮ Auburn Trail	㊱ Dingmans Falls
	⑰ Eternal Flame Falls	㊸ Tillman's Ravine
	⑱ Watkins Glen	㊽ Cattus Island
Summer	① Shadmoor State Park	⑯ Niagara Whirlpool
	⑥ Black Creek Preserve	⑲ Taughannock Falls
	⑧ Indian Ladder Trail	㉕ Ohiopyle Slides
	⑩ Cobble Hill	㊸ Tillman's Ravine
	⑫ Stone Valley	
Fall	② Harriman State Park	㉚ Rimrock Trail
	④ Dover Stone Church	㉛ Kinzua Bridge
	⑤ Lake Minnewaska	㉜ Otter Point
	⑥ Black Creek Preserve	㉞ Ricketts Glen
	⑧ Indian Ladder Trail	㊲ Buttermilk and
	⑩ Cobble Hill	Luke's Falls
	⑫ Stone Valley	㊵ Pyramid Mountain
	⑬ Bald Mountain	㊶ Van Slyke Castle
	⑮ Auburn Trail	㊷ Pochuck Suspension
	⑱ Watkins Glen	Bridge
	㉘ Tamarack Trail	㊻ Goat Hill Overlook
		50 Cape May

PREPARING FOR YOUR ADVENTURE

This guide is a starter pack to a life full of exploration with your young ones. One day, your adventurers could be calling you up to ask if you want to join them to summit New York's Mount Marcy. My own father took me out on hikes all over the country from toddlerhood, inspiring my thirst for outdoor adventure—flash forward a couple decades and it was him coming with me on all the hikes in this guide. One day, perhaps we'll tackle the aforementioned Appalachian Trail, which powers its way from Springer Mountain, Georgia, to Mount Katahdin, Maine. Maybe your family will too. In the meantime, work together to taste what each spectacularly diverse region has to offer and note which ones you want to return to in the future.

INDIVIDUAL ADVENTURE PROFILES

Each of the fifty adventure profiles includes a basic trail map and information on the species of plants and wildlife, points of historic interest, and geological features that you may see on the trail. Allowing children to navigate using the maps and elevation guides, reading the hike and species descriptions, and looking for each featured item in the scavenger hunts puts the building blocks of adventure in their hands. Marking journeys on the map with points of interest gives relevance and context to kids' surroundings, so encourage them to note anything that stood out even if it's not noted in the book. You'll burst with pride when kids start to teach *you* what a lollipop loop is versus an out and back, are able to gauge whether they feel like just kickin' it on a hike with 200 feet of elevation gain or tackling 1,000 feet, and make decisions about their own adventure. Each description is written for both you and the kids, so encourage them to read to themselves or out loud to you.

∧ Trail signs can range from simple to detailed

Elevation profile, length, type of trail, and time

An elevation profile is a line that sketches the general arch of the up and down during a hike. You'll notice a few are almost completely flat, and some are nearly a triangle. The elevation gain is how many feet you'll gain from start to finish; so even if it rolls up and then down again, if it says 300 feet

∧ You will encounter all sorts of trails on your adventures

that will be the total number of feet you'll have to walk up from the trail-head to the summit. No adventure is less than a half mile (too short to call a real excursion) or more than 5 miles (inaccessible for many of our younger or newer adventurers). The length of these hikes should give you plenty of time to enjoy the outing before anyone gets too tired. Embracing shorter trails translates into more time to savor them. Some of the routes are shorter versions of a longer route and modified for kids—be sure to check out the land agency's map of whichever area you're visiting in case you want to explore more. Along with the length of the trail, I note whether the adventure is an out and back, a loop, or a lollipop loop.

 An out and back has a clear final destination and turnaround point, and you'll cross back over what you've already discovered.

 A loop provides brand-new territory the whole way around.

 A lollipop is a straight line with a mini-loop at the end, like reaching a lake and then circling it, and heading back.

Talking with kids about the type of trail you're planning to hike will help young adventurers know what to expect. The estimated hike time includes time for exploration, and each adventurer's mileage may vary. Always give yourselves the delight of a relaxing hike with plenty of time to stop and play with a pile of fun-looking rocks, have leaf-boat races on a stream, or sketch a cool plant or animal.

Level of difficulty

Often, when you research "kid-friendly" hikes, you'll find relatively sterile, flat, paved trails. While these are perfect for first-time hikers or toddlers, I know kids are capable of true adventure, so the hikes in this book are all true-blue hikes and adventures. It's important to note that these are kid-centric ratings; what's labeled as a "challenging" trail in this guide may not appear to be so challenging for a seasoned adult hiker. It can be fun to create your own rating for a trail when you're finished. "Did that feel like a level one, two, or three to you? Why?" Talking about it can help you understand an individual kid's adventure limits or help them seek new challenges. None of the trails in this book are paved (at least not all the way). Some are level and smooth, but due to the geological history of New York, Pennsylvania, and New Jersey, most have some combination of rocks and roots. There will be notes if a trail has exposed ledges or viewpoints where you'll want to hold small hands. Rocky terrain will cry for some sturdy shoes, and you'll want to have a bead on how wet, muddy, or snowy it may be to choose which pair will be best for your child. It can help if you check reviews on AllTrails.com to get recent conditions and different families' opinions of the difficulty—you can also call the office of a nearby ranger station. While scouting these trails with my family, I saw many walking toddlers, strollers of every tire type imaginable, and baby backpacks on even the most challenging trails. I also spotted a couple sport strollers on moderately rocky trails with exposed roots. Use the information here to make informed decisions—every lead adventurer is different.

The adventures are rated as follows:

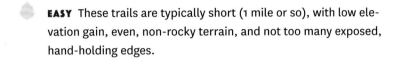 **EASY** These trails are typically short (1 mile or so), with low elevation gain, even, non-rocky terrain, and not too many exposed, hand-holding edges.

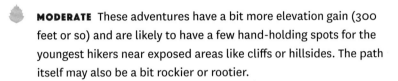 **MODERATE** These adventures have a bit more elevation gain (300 feet or so) and are likely to have a few hand-holding spots for the youngest hikers near exposed areas like cliffs or hillsides. The path itself may also be a bit rockier or rootier.

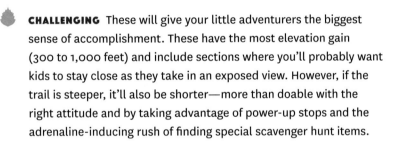 **CHALLENGING** These will give your little adventurers the biggest sense of accomplishment. These have the most elevation gain (300 to 1,000 feet) and include sections where you'll probably want kids to stay close as they take in an exposed view. However, if the trail is steeper, it'll also be shorter—more than doable with the right attitude and by taking advantage of power-up stops and the adrenaline-inducing rush of finding special scavenger hunt items.

Get there

When I was seven, my dad took our family out for our first off-roading experience in a small white Toyota pickup in the California desert. Our truck was promptly lodged between two rocks and got towed out six hours later. Although that experience built some character and an adventurous spirit in me, these kinds of roads are not included in this guide. These adventures have all been road tested at least once and specifically target trailheads with fairly easy access—meaning minimal dirt, gravel, or pothole-strewn roads. I'll leave those to our seasoned adventurers.

Your region is big, folks. Over 109,340 square miles over New York, Pennsylvania, and New Jersey. This guide is meant to be a promotion for the diverse and beautiful areas all around you. I hope that you and your children flip through and dream of one day taking a road trip to the east-ernmost point of New York on Long Island or to see an eternal flame in the rocks near Buffalo, for just two epic examples. Car rides are a necessity to reach this amazing buffet of hikes available to you, and I hope you embrace the special family time that road trips can offer your crew.

Of course, you have your screen of choice, but consider a few fun ways to make the hours fly by fast, such as riddles, the A–Z game (you claim a point every time you see something that starts with the next letter of the alphabet), audiobooks, call-and-response-type camp songs (ulti-matecampresource.com/camp-songs), nature journaling, and just good old-fashioned conversation. Always be ready to roll down windows for fresh air and encourage your little riders to look at the horizon if they start to get carsick. I encourage you to always stop by visitor centers, make the most of every trip, and consider finding somewhere nearby to camp to enjoy the area longer.

Basic directions to the trailhead are listed with each adventure, along with a *case-sensitive* link to Google Maps you can drop directly into your smartphone browser. Be sure to do this before you head out, while you are certain to have coverage. You can also get free highway maps mailed to you or printed, which can be helpful and educational for your little co-pilot (check the tourism websites for each state: iloveny.com, visitpa.com, and visitnj.gov). Before leaving home, you and your adventurer can geek out on Google Earth or turn on satellite view in Google Maps to follow your route (and sometimes even your trail) step by step.

There's something magical about maps, and each map in this guide was carefully designed with kids in mind to be touched, traced, and held out in front of them to understand their surroundings. Encourage your kids to understand the difference between roads, highways, and interstate freeways. We've simplified the maps so kids can focus on the land agencies they'll be visiting, the closest towns with grub stops, and the larger cities nearby. Hopefully, while they adventure with you, they'll start to build a sixth sense for using maps. Ask them navigation questions. How long will

∧ Once you find the adventure location, the trail will often have helpful ways to get where you're going

this adventure take, do you think? Where does that river start, and how is it related to the ocean? How many turns will we need to make? What's our next highway? Any cities nearby? Any fun names you can see? Just asking questions can encourage curiosity and leadership in your young adventurers.

Restrooms

We can't have a hiking book for kids without chatting about bathrooms. Many trails have pit toilets or developed toilets right at the parking lot. If not, plan on a restroom stop in the nearest town or gas station on your way in and on your way out. Discuss appropriate trail bathroom etiquette with your kids as well, such as heading safely off the trail, away from water, and properly covering or burying waste should the need arise. Pack your adventure bag with what you need to be comfortable, such as a Ziploc bag with toilet paper. Don't leave any toilet paper behind to spoil someone else's experience; make sure to pack it back out.

Parking and fees

Your main goal, lead adventurers, is to get out on the trail. If thinking about how to park and pay gets your boot laces knotted up, rest assured that as long as you have some cash in the glove compartment, the team will be just fine. All the trailheads listed here have a parking lot or pullout and some sort of trail sign indicating where you are and whether you need a parking pass or permit. For some, you'll need to plan ahead and get a day or annual pass before you get to the trailhead. Others have self-service pay stations at the trailhead—either those accepting credit cards or an "iron ranger" with a slot in it for a fee envelope with cash or check—and you'll affix the pass to your car. Many parking lots are free, though, and each is noted. Pennsylvania has no entrance or day-use fees in state parks but does charge for overnight camping and other activities. New Jersey and New York state parks have a broad spectrum of fees, depending on the day and park, but offer annual passes.

Treat yourself

The guide lists nearby cafes and restaurants for good, quick bites to reward yourselves, in part so you can plan whether you need to pack substantial snacks or just a few for sustenance on the trail. These are road-tested bakeries, ice cream shops, burger joints, and family-friendly breweries with notable items or spaces that your kids will enjoy. The northern mid-Atlantic's bounty of tomato pies, pizza logs, wings, cheesesteaks, hoagies, and tubbers of ice cream are calling!

Managing agencies

I've listed the name of the agency that manages each hiking trail, along with its telephone number and pertinent social media handles. Before heading out, it's a good idea to check on current conditions, including weather, roads, wildlife sightings, and any hazards that haven't been cleared or fixed. The folks on the other end are often rangers and are generally thrilled to share information about their trails. They can also connect you to botanists, geologists, historians, and other experts. I received fast and enthusiastic responses from many of the rangers behind the Facebook pages of these parks—involve your kids and encourage them to say hello and ask about conditions or a lingering question from the trail.

∧ Blazes and discs mark the way
on most of the trails in this guide

Following the trail

In this region, colorful blazes on trees and rocks mark the way along most trails. While I have made every effort to pick straightforward trails that are hard to get lost on, it's good to build the habit of always looking for the next blaze and question your path if you haven't seen one in a while. In our family, it's a coveted prize to be the first person to see each blaze. Another good habit to encourage in your kids is taking a moment at each power-up stop to note the landmarks around them and check to see what comes next on the map. These skills will help them out when they get older and graduate from this guide to more difficult trails. Give a hug to a tree with a blaze on it and send a mental thank-you to the land agencies that maintain the blazes and make outdoor adventure possible for us all.

Scavenger hunts

The scavenger hunt included with each adventure invites you to look for specific fungi, plants, animals, minerals, and historical items of interest. You'll find descriptions and photos of trees, leaves, flowers, seeds, cones, bark, nuts, wildlife or animal tracks, fur and feathers, rocks and geological features, historically significant landmarks or artifacts, natural features such as lakes, rivers, and waterfalls, or culturally significant spots that appear on each trail. Entries have questions to ponder or activities to try, and, when applicable, you can dig into the scientific genus and species and learn why a plant or animal is called what it is. Encourage kids to "preview" what they might see on the trail, and if they think they've found it, pull out the book to match. Take it up a notch and encourage them to make their *own* scavenger hunt—write down five things they think they might see on the trail today, from very basic (at least five trees) to very specific (five eastern white pine cones on the ground).

IDENTIFYING WHAT YOU FIND

Identifying the bounty of species in the wild involves using clues from size, leaves, bark, flowers, and habitat. Work with kids to ask questions that will move them from general identification (Is it a conifer/evergreen or a deciduous tree?) to the specifics (What shape are the leaves? What species is this?). The species of trees, shrubs, mushrooms, wildflowers, and animals listed in the scavenger hunts were chosen because you should be able to find them with ease and because there's something interesting about them that might appeal to children. You may not find every species on the trail every time, however. It's best to adopt the attitude of considering it a win when you do find one, and to present those you can't find as something to look forward to the next time.

Tristan Gooley, British author of *The Natural Navigator*, encourages kids to look for "keys" as they walk on trails: "Keys are small families of clues and signs, if we focus on them repeatedly, it can give us a sixth sense." Start noticing where the sun is when you start and end and where the natural features (hills, mountains) are around you. Use a compass (there's probably one on your smartphone) to start understanding direction and building this natural sixth sense Gooley speaks of.

When you find a particularly interesting species that's not mentioned in the scavenger hunt, have kids either sketch it or take a photo of it. Remind them to look it up later, either in a printed field guide to the region or on a specialty website such as wildflowersearch.com or iNaturalist.org. Including basic descriptions and the name of the region in the search will help kids find their treasure in online field guides. LeafSnap.com and the Seek app by iNaturalist are also great for creating species treasure hunts on the trail.

Look at the things you encounter from different scales and different angles and different parts. Take a tree: you have a really large organism, and you might need to stand really far away to see a picture of it. But look closer—and find the fruit on the ground, look at the bark, look at the leaves. Think of all the different characteristics that can help you learn what it is, why it lives where it is. Start recognizing all the pieces of an organism and thinking about how to capture those photographically if you want to share that record with the world. Try to find the part of the thing that is most unique-looking and fill the frame with that for a nice, clear photo.

—Carrie Seltzer, iNaturalist

If you're ready to level up everyone's identification skills, join the Native Plant Trust, the Northeast Mycological Federation (for mushrooms), or a botanical society such as New York Native Plant Society (nanps.org), Pennsylvania Native Plant Society (panativeplantsociety.org), or Native Plant Society of New Jersey (npsnj.org). All have great Facebook groups, newsletters, or online forums where you can share photos of a species you can't identify. The USA Phenology Network (usanpn.org) allows kids to contribute to actual science by entering their observation of seasonal changes into a nationwide database,

∧ There are many treasures to find on the trail

and it has a cool Junior Phenologist Program plus kid-friendly resources to boot. Joining your local chapter also means getting invited to their fun group hikes, with themes from wildflowers to fungi and everything in between. You're also exposing your kids to the power of a community resource in which everyone is passionate about nature and science and wants to help one another.

This region is a very cool place to explore rocks and geology and you'll notice some amazing sights in the adventures here. While encountering the amazing colors, folds, and structures, encourage children to think about the rock's general cycle—its evolution from igneous to metamorphic to sedimentary—and how it builds up in deposits over time.

Use the scavenger hunts to build a familiarity with different types of rocks. Ask questions—what does the texture of the rock look like? What color is it? Does it feel heavy or light? Is it hard or soft? Does it break easily? Join a regional geological society like the New York State Geological

The rock that forms the core of the rugged mountains of the Adirondacks is some of the oldest rock on Earth (nearly 1.1 billion years old) and was once covered by layers of sedimentary rock that were scoured away from ice sheets and glaciers. The geology of the region is diverse, and the ancient stories are revealed strikingly by the varied topography and landscapes—this is evident all around the region. My interest in geology began with digging in the backyard of my childhood home and collecting rocks from everywhere I went, including hiking trips to the Adirondacks, Catskills, and Appalachians.

—Gregory C. Wyka, New York state geologist

Association (nysga-online.org), Geological Association of New Jersey (ganj. org), or Pittsburgh Geological Society (pittsburghgeologicalsociety.org) for newsletters, group hikes, and community opportunities. Rockhounding and personal collecting is allowed at several of the adventure sites and can begin to spur an interest in geology and science. You can even join the National Speleological Society if you're interested in caves.

Historical items

Join your local historical society to start to identify items of historical interest on your trails. Each state has its own historical society with resources and an email and phone number to ask questions: New York's is nyhistory.org, Pennsylvania's are portal.hsp.org and pa-history.org, and New Jersey's is njhistory.org. Parents can foster inquiry with each hike.

∧ How is this 1776 map of New York, Pennsylvania, and New Jersey different from today's map? How might the map look different in the future?

This is a golden chance for parents to share what they know with their children. If parents can take time to research various aspects of trail history, they can bring more excitement to time with their children. By trading stories and questions, before you know it, you become mutual teachers and students on the trails you have learned to love. Every trail has its own story to share, and every landmark from the earth to the trees to the sky and everything in between can be something touched by your curiosity. You are all making your own history in sharing a path walked upon by dinosaurs, Native Americans, wildlife, and many different explorers. This creates a beautiful family memory to be shared with friends and neighbors and even future generations!

—Alan Delozier, New Jersey state historian

POWER-UP STOPS

Liz Thomas has hiked over 20,000 miles and is a former speed record holder for the Appalachian Trail. Her biggest tip for young adventurers learning to build stamina is, "Understand your body. Kids are just figuring out how to read their bodies. You can think of your body as having gauges and you're the pilot at the front of the plane. Your goal is to keep your gauges (hydration, exposure, food) in the happy zone." She even sets reminders on her watch to drink and eat as she walks from sunrise to sunset. As lead adventurers, you'll be keeping a close eye on these gauges but also helping kids recognize, anticipate, and power through them.

For each adventure, I note key places that serve as mini milestones or power-up stops. Be sure to pack snacks for kids to eat at these stops to keep blood sugar, energy levels, and mood high. Remember that this amount of physical activity may be challenging for littles. Often, these power-up stops are at points of interest: fun bridges, switchbacks before a small hill,

or overlooking a viewpoint. Stopping for a moment can fuel you up, give you a chance to listen to the wind or animals around you, watch what's going on in the woods, and prepare you for the larger goal of finishing the adventure itself.

Power-ups can also be great for a nursing mom or bottle-feeding dad or for tending to other little ones' needs, as well as for question-based games like "I Spy." As the lead adventurer, you can use these stops

< **Bridges make great places to relax and explore**

for inspiration, play, questions, games, and riddles. Encourage your kids to do the same. Don't underestimate the power of choosing a special snack to serve as a particular motivator on tough ascents or rainy days.

Watch how kids' interaction with nature changes—from perceiving it only through their senses to experiencing it through imagination and fantasy. A toddler in a parent's backpack is enough to cultivate that sense; stopping for a while to explore a fairy house is always a good idea with a three- or four-year-old. As they get older, children begin to appreciate the joy of overcoming challenging terrain.

ADVENTURE BAG, SUPPLIES, AND SAFETY

Start your kids on a lifelong habit of packing an adventure bag, whether it's the smallest satchel or the largest consumer-grade backpack they can hold. The art of having everything you need with you without being too burdened is key to having a good time on the trail. All these adventures are short enough that even if you did pack too much, the weight won't jeopardize your enjoyment levels too much.

 NAVIGATION In addition to the maps in this book, consider investing in a compass and full trail map of the area. Make sure your smartphone is fully charged, with offline maps available and the compass feature handy. My family likes to carry an extra portable battery for our phones.

 HYDRATION Bring plenty of water for everyone and remember to drink along the way.

 NUTRITION Consider the length of the trail and the amount and type of snacks you'll need to keep the train going.

FIRE Pack a lighter or matchbook for emergencies.

 FIRST AID KIT This can range from a small first aid kit with essentials such as bandages and aspirin to much heftier options with space blankets. Consider what you want your car stocked with and what you want on the trail with you.

 TOOLS A small knife or multi-tool goes a long way in the woods.

 ILLUMINATION Did you explore just a wee bit too long and dusk is approaching? A simple headlamp, flashlight, or even your phone's flashlight can help lead the way.

 SUN AND INSECT PROTECTION If it's an exposed trail, consider sunglasses and sunscreen or hats for you and the kids. In summer and when things get warm, many trails may have mosquitoes, flies, and ticks, so be prepared with your favorite method of repelling them.

 SHELTER You may want a space blanket or small tarp in your adventure bag in case of emergency.

 INSULATION Check the weather together and decide the type of protection and warmth you want to bring. A second layer is always a good idea—breezes can chill even the warmest of days.

Fun items to have on hand might include a nature journal and pen or pencil, hand lens, binoculars, a bug jar for capturing and releasing spiders and insects, a camera, a super-special treat for when you reach the top of something, a container for a special mushroom or pine cone, and even a favorite figurine or toy that your littles are currently enamored with so they can use it to interact with that tree stump up ahead. Wet wipes, toilet paper, and Ziploc bags are also recommended. First-timer? Join the local chapter of a hiking group like Hike it Baby or the Sierra Club to hike with your peers and learn the ropes of packing.

Hikes present challenges around fatigue, getting thirsty, and sometimes getting bruised by branches and rocks. So whining can cut into the fun. The challenge, then, is for parents to both validate and encourage—to not be the army sergeant nor the coddler. Bruising happens . . . it's the tone of the parent that matters. [As your child developmentally gets older, around nine or ten] more serious hiking is attainable. Each mountain can become your child's friend if only one climbs and gets to know a lifelong love that rivals lifelong friendships for satisfaction and meaning. Most mountains worth climbing have several trails to choose from, each with its own special challenges and wondrous features. To get to know a mountain or, better yet, a mountain range, can be one of the great pleasures in life.

—W. George Scarlett, senior lecturer on child development, Tufts University

While it may be handy for you to navigate to trailheads using your smartphone, remember that many wilderness areas have spotty cell service. As a general safety practice for hiking with kids, always tell a third party where you are going and when you expect to be back and remember to tell anyone who may need to get ahold of you that you're not certain of cell coverage in the area. If you adventure a lot, you might want to consider an affordable satellite GPS, like those made by Garmin, that allows you to send texts from areas that don't have cell service. On the trail itself, every lead adventurer will have his or her own comfort level with safety, and you'll determine when your children will need hand-holding or reminders to stay close as you get near tricky terrain, exposed edges, or water.

It's a given in the northern mid-Atlantic's diversity of climates that adverse weather conditions can arrive seemingly out of nowhere. Teaching awareness and common sense and fostering an attitude of "there's no bad weather, only the wrong clothing" in these situations will go a long way toward creating an adventurous and resilient child. You can model this "love the unlovable" attitude by remaining upbeat and playful as lead adventurer;

< **Poison ivy (*Toxicodendron radicans*)**

you'll be amazed at how quickly their attention will turn back to the trail and its wonders.

In addition to weather, poison ivy is a common hazard lurking in the woods of these states. Fortunately, once you can identify it, you'll be able to spot it with almost infrared vision. Touching this plant causes a blistering rash in most people. Remember the warning, "Leaves of three, let it be"—although the plant can grow as a spreading vine or a low or upright shrub, its groups of three leaflets make it easy to identify. New leaves start out red, then fade to a yellowy bronze before turning fully green in summer and bright red, orange, or yellow in late summer and fall.

Aside from deer on the road, the northern mid-Atlantic doesn't have much in the way of large, dangerous animals. American black bears (*Ursus americanus*), coyotes (*Canis latrans*), and bobcats (*Lynx rufus*) are shy of humans and you're quite unlikely to encounter them on hikes. If it is a possibility, trailheads will often have information on animals in the area and reminders of how to take precautions. If you do see a bear, try not to freak out—simply hold your ground, make loud noises, and slowly back away—as they are not aggressive. Do not run and never get between a bear and her cubs. By helping kids be aware on the trail, looking for signs of wildlife and understanding what to do during an encounter, you can create a lifelong safety skillset for adventuring. Please also be aware of all trailhead signs; as mentioned previously, if hunting is permitted in fall and winter, you'll want to wear bright orange on your head and body—we'll call out specific trails where this applies, but it's always good to check ahead of time for your destination.

The most dangerous critter in the region is arguably *Ixodes scapularis*, the deer tick or blacklegged tick, which can spread Lyme disease. Knowledge of ticks, tick-borne diseases, and tick prevention and safety is essential and goes hand in hand with hiking. Ticks don't fly or jump; they attach to animals that come into direct contact with them, then they feed on the blood (yours, your dog's, other mammals). They love shrubby, grassy areas—be sure to stick to the center of the trail and don't go off-trail. Before a hike, consider wearing light clothing so you can quickly spot any ticks that have hitched a ride. Consider treating your clothes with 0.5 percent permethrin or 20–30 percent DEET (be sure to apply for your children, avoiding eyes, nose, and mouth). Make full-body tick checks a part of your hiking routine when you get back to the car. Be sure to check under your arms, behind your knees and ears, and between your toes. Shower or bath time at home provides another chance for a full-body check. If you find a tick, remove it with tweezers or a tick removal kit as close to your skin as possible. Don't handle it with your bare hands, clean the area with soap and water, and call your doctor. Ticks can be found in almost any season so it's best to always perform checks.

∧ Ticks are small and difficult to spot, so be sure to check carefully for them after every hike

NATURE JOURNALING

I received my first nature journal in Sydney, Australia, on my first night as a National Geographic Fellow with a group of students and teachers from around the world. It was leather bound and bursting with empty pages just begging to be doodled and documented on (I now have six and counting).

Catherine Hughes, retired head of the *National Geographic Kids* magazine education team, gently guided us with a few key maxims for nature journaling:

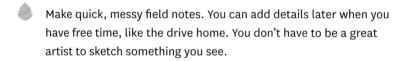 Make quick, messy field notes. You can add details later when you have free time, like the drive home. You don't have to be a great artist to sketch something you see.

Sketch the map of the adventure that day.

Personalize it. Did someone say something funny? What was the most unique thing that happened on the adventure?

Use it like a scrapbook. Add any trail brochure or ticket to your journal to remember your adventure.

Jaedon sketches the tracks of a seagull in the sand

A great trail is a story—it has a beginning, a true climax or crux, then an end, whether that's back the way you came or at the completion of a loop. As you review your outings with young adventurers, encourage them to feel the story of the trail. How did they like the beginning? What was the climax? How did it end? What characters (plants, rock formations, animals) stood out to them? A fun after-hike activity is taking your nature journal and writing a fictional account of what happened on the trail, making the landscape come alive in a whole new way.

One of my favorite techniques is to take one flower, branch, or leaf and draw it from several different angles. Each time you rotate, you'll notice new details you didn't see before. Or, you can create interesting compositions by drawing and layering multiple stages of a plant, like buds, fallen petals, and full blooms.

—Maggie Enterrios, author of *Nature Observer: A Guided Journal*

Consider picking out a small blank journal for kids to bring along in their adventure bags. When you stop for lunch at your destination, at power-up stops, on the ride home, or later that night, encourage your little adventurers to create drawings of things they saw, document their observations of trees or animals, or press leaves or flowers.

DIGITAL CONNECTIONS

The social media accounts of many of the agencies that manage public lands in the region are quite active, and they can be a great way for kids to use technology to enhance their experience in nature. They can ask pre- or post-adventure questions about conditions or flora and fauna, and the forums can be wonderful vehicles for sharing images you snapped—for both you and your little adventurer. Search the location on Instagram for recent photos and be sure to geo-tag yours to contribute to other hikers' searches as well. Enhance the journey and encourage them to define what really stood out to them about the experience with a coauthored trip report on one of these sites:

 Local options like New York/New Jersey Trail Conference Dive deep into specific states—kids can help the community by adding photos and comments after their hikes.

 AllTrails.com This a crowd-sourced database of hikes built by a community of 4 million registered members that includes reviews, user-uploaded photos, and downloadable maps.

 wildflowersearch.com This site has many good tools for identifying flowers. Some are as simple to use as uploading a photo and asking it to scan a database for you. It also has up-to-date lists of species in bloom.

 iNaturalist.org and Seek by iNaturalist This web- and app-based online community allows you to share your species observations with other naturalists around the world. It's also a great place to post a question if you can't identify something you found.

 Geocaching.com or the Geocaching app Geocaches are treasures hidden by other people with GPS coordinates posted online. If you're heading out on one of the adventures, check the website or app to see if anyone has hidden a treasure along the trail. If they have, you can use your phone to navigate to it, find it, exchange a treasure item or sign the log, and re-hide it where you found it. About twelve years ago I hid one on a trail, and it's been found more than 500 times!

For younger children, it's important to engage their emotions and their senses, above and beyond identifying plants or animals by name. Rachel Carson advises that children are likely to remember an expression of excitement about seeing something in the natural world, especially when expressed by an adult companion. One of the interesting and almost universal features of wonder is how it often involves one person exclaiming "Look!" to another person. It's almost instinctive. That sense of shared excitement is likely to make an impression on younger children.

—Lisa Sideris, Indiana University

SMARTPHONES

You may have picked up this book to find ways of distracting kids from their phones. Not using a phone at all during your adventures can be fun and appropriate, and you probably already know where you stand on the issue of screen time, but if you want to try to strike a balance, letting kids use their phone on the trail to take a picture of an interesting flower, navigate with a digital compass app, use the audio app to capture a birdsong, or share their pictures of the hike on the state forest's Instagram can be a conscientious way to bridge technology and outdoor time (just be sure the phone is put away more than it is out).

< Kids love using digital photography to capture scenic views; let them be the official photographers on your hikes

∧ There are many spots for rock hopping on these adventures

SHOWING RESPECT FOR NATURE

There are 40 million lovely people in this region, and enjoying and protecting its land will be key to conserving its beauty for generations to come. We are inspiring stewards—the more we are out there understanding and delighting in the natural world with our families, the more we and our little adventurers want to take care of it in the future. Some of the beautiful areas in this guide are also the most remote and precious. You're doing the most important thing you can to keep these states beautiful—taking your kids outside.

You can't help but feel a part of something larger when you and your kids get yourselves on top of a fire tower or hike up, over, and around eighteen waterfalls on one trail. By simply noticing and beginning to identify features, flora, and fauna in nature you're creating a sense of respect and appreciation. Model and embrace the "Leave No Trace" ethos (see LNT.org for more great ideas) on each and every trail. Be diligent with snack wrappers and the flotsam and jetsam of your adventure bag. Be sure to always stay on the trail and avoid trampling vegetation and disturbing wildlife to ensure that everyone and everything can share the adventure.

The scavenger hunts will be asking kids to act as young naturalists; to notice, touch, and play with nature around them in a safe and gentle way. For the most part, try not to take a leaf or flower off a growing plant, but rather collect and play with items that are already on the ground. Manipulate them, stack them, create art with them, trace them in journals—but then leave them to be used by the other creatures on the trail, from the fungi decomposing a leaf to another kid walking down the trail tomorrow. Invite your kids to see if they can help with citizen science by reporting observations back to ranger stations, cleaning up trash, and volunteering to maintain trails. Many of these wilderness areas and public lands were created with the help of state leaders, and you're creating the next generation of conservationists simply by getting kids out in them.

ADVENTURES IN
NEW YORK

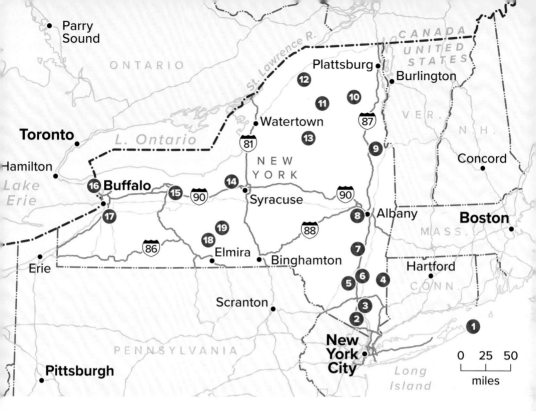

Adventurers, we begin in the Empire State, which became a state in 1788. The state motto is "Excelsior!" Translated from Latin, this means "ever upward," so let's continue to adventure, ever upward! We'll begin in the village of Montauk on Long Island, then head north up the Hudson River to check out a mine at Harriman State Park. We'll explore a cave with a waterfall *inside* it, walk on boardwalks at the Audubon Society, and cross a suspension bridge at Black Creek Preserve. In the Catskill Mountains, we'll look over the site where a famous hotel once stood. Then it's around Lake Minnewaska and into the Appalachian Mountains—we're heading upstate! We'll stop by Shelving Rock Mountain, then make our way to Lake Placid and use ropes to climb Cobble Hill. Things flatten out a bit as we reach the Erie-Ontario lowlands and follow a boardwalk around a marsh, walk an old railroad to watch birds, and view a natural whirlpool at the Canadian border. Then it's south for a flame that has been burning a *long* time, and one of the eleven Finger Lakes to see the largest waterfall in the region. Are you ready? Excelsior!

1

HIKE TO HOODOOS AT
SHADMOOR STATE PARK

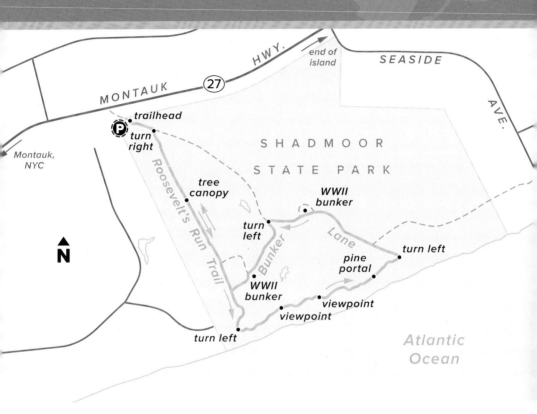

YOUR ADVENTURE

Adventurers, imagine the Montaukett people living here centuries ago, then skip forward to 1898, when President Teddy Roosevelt and his Rough Riders quarantined here due to malaria after the Spanish-American War. Start on the wide, sandy path and take your first right on Roosevelt's Run. The trail narrows a bit—spray up with your favorite bug repellent, be sure not to go off-trail, and do a tick check at the end. Walk under the beautiful tree

LENGTH

1.3-mile

lollipop loop

ELEV [FT]

400–

0–

Elevation
Gain

45ft.

DISTANCE [MI]

1   2   3   4

HIKE + EXPLORE 1 hour

DIFFICULTY Easy—flat, short, and beautiful. Use caution at the cliff's edges, be alert for ticks, and be sure to follow the map as there are a few trail offshoots.

SEASON Year-round. Seals can be seen in winter and monarch butterflies arrive in fall. Summer brings pink gerardia blooms, as well as ticks and chiggers—always check after your hike.

GET THERE Take Montauk Highway / NY-27 northeast through Montauk. Turn right at the sign for Shadmoor State Park.

Google Maps: bit.ly/timbershadmoor

RESTROOMS None at trailhead, but plenty in Montauk

FEE None

TREAT YOURSELF Montauk Bake Shoppe is just off Montauk Highway on The Plaza. Get an egg roll or lobster cookie to go and eat on the beach.

Shadmoor State Park; New York State Parks, Recreation and Historic Preservation (631) 668-3781 | Twitter @NYStateParks Facebook @NYStateParks

Your view of the
Atlantic Ocean

canopy and pass Bunker Lane (for now). Soon the canopy will open to full sky and the Atlantic Ocean. Power up here, noticing the hoodoo rock shapes around you, then turn left to follow the ledge. It is fenced but be careful—hold small hands. Take the trail to the right to pass through two viewpoints and then the pine tree portal. Arrive at a vast opening where you'll see a route heading left. Take that, stay straight at the next junction, and you'll find yourself at the first WWII artillery bunker. Continue on and follow Bunker Lane to your left, which will take you to the next bunker. Another left and you can reconnect with Roosevelt's Run; turn right and head back to the parking lot. Consider camping at Hither Hills State Park.

SCAVENGER HUNT

Shadbush

Can you find this park's namesake? It blooms white flowers in spring, but its taco-shaped leaves line the path all times of year. If you find a leaf on the ground, prepare a "dirt taco" for your hiking buddy. Shadbush is also known as serviceberry.

< *Amelanchier* in bloom

Seasonal special: sandplain gerardia

Watch for this endangered and rare species blooming in summer or fall. Look closely: its pink flowers poke out with purple dots in the middle. Think about why some plant species become threatened. What do you think made this one endangered?

Agalinis acuta is an endangered species >

Black cherry

Look for this tree as you begin your hike. It is deciduous (drops its leaves in fall) and so much is made from this species of tree, including cherry cough syrup from its bark. Look for its white flowers in spring and cherries in the late summer.

< *Prunus serotina* at the trail's start

Hoodoo

Once the trail hits the beach, take your nature journal out and try to sketch the patterns of the hoodoos. All of this was deposited by a glacier 22,000 years ago. Wind and water still sculpt these—when you get home, take some mud, Play-Doh, or sand and try to "weather" them into a shape like these.

Hoodoos come in wacky, weird shapes >

WWII concrete bunker

As you look out from the bottom of the bunker, visualize spotting the American clipper ship that ran aground here in 1858—the *John Milton*. When an unwelcome vessel was spotted, information on the location of the vessel would be forwarded to Camp Hero, where 16-inch guns were located. If necessary, the guns would be trained on the location and . . . *boom!*

< Imagine peering out from this WWII bunker in 1944

2

BE A SWAMP THING AT HARRIMAN STATE PARK

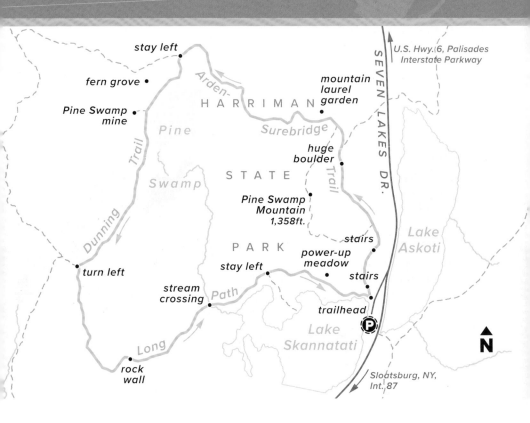

YOUR ADVENTURE

Adventurers, up, down, and around we go on the historical homeland of the Munsee. Start to the right on the red-blazed Arden-Surebridge Trail, heading counterclockwise and gradually climbing up and down over boulders and in a huge canopy of trees. Climb a couple sets of stairs and find the biggest boulder. Power up there, then head downhill. Cross through the mountain laurel garden and eventually turn left onto the yellow Dunning

LENGTH

3.3-mile

loop

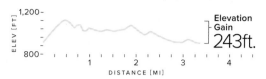

ELEV [FT]

1,200–

800–

Elevation Gain
243ft.

1   2   3   4

DISTANCE [MI]

HIKE + EXPLORE 2.5 hours

DIFFICULTY Challenging—on the longer side with rocky and rooty spots up and down on hills. Be bear-aware, watch out for rattlesnakes, and check for ticks when you're finished.

SEASON Year-round. Roads may be closed in winter and trail can be icy, so check beforehand.

GET THERE North of New York City, get on Palisades Interstate Parkway. Take Exit 14 for Willow Grove Road and turn left. Merge onto Kanawauke Road then take the first exit at the traffic circle onto Seven Lakes Drive. Parking for Lake Skannatati will be at a sharp turn on your left.

Google Maps: bit.ly/timberpineswamp

RESTROOMS None

FEE None

TREAT YOURSELF Grab whoopie pies, cookies, and breakfast sandos to go at Dottie Audrey's Bakery Kitchen just off NY-17 in Tuxedo Park.

Harriman State Park; New York State Parks, Recreation and Historic Preservation
(845) 947-2444
Facebook @Harriman-State-Park-316240675169741

Just below the mine is the Pine Swamp

Trail. Look to your left—that's the Pine Swamp, a mix of open water, peaty bog, and shrub swamp. Peat is formed by the partial decay of plant material and the bog is home to beavers, lots of frogs and turtles, and aquatic insects. Pass a fern grove on the right and watch for a small trail up the hill. Carefully climb the hill and go left once you're on top. Step carefully and find the 30-foot mine shaft. Observe from afar then head back to continue on the main trail. Soon the swamp ends; turn left on the aqua-blazed Long Path. Cross a stream, stay to the left, do one final power-up at a meadow, and find yourself back at the beginning. Consider camping just down the road at Beaver Pond Campground.

SCAVENGER HUNT

Pine Swamp mine

This passageway was tunneled into the hillside in the 1830s by brothers Robert and Peter Parrott. The mine produced iron that was used to make the famous Parrott gun for the Civil War. It closed in the 1880s. The park currently discourages off-trail exploration of the mine, so check with a ranger before taking a closer look.

Shaft opening of the Pine Swamp mine >

Mountain laurel

Look for the mountain laurel garden on your way up, surrounding you on both sides of the trail. It will be blooming in the late spring and early summer, but you can't miss its leaves year-round.

< *Kalmia latifolia*

Hickory leaves and nut

Look for this tree's alternate (on both sides of the stem) leaves. It produces long male catkin flowers and smaller female flowers in spring. The nut ripens in fall; you might find a hollow shell like this one, cracked and snacked on by a squirrel.

Hickory leaves and a cracked nutshell >

Black rat snake

New York is home to seventeen snake species, and one you might catch a glimpse of is the harmless black rat snake, the largest of those species, which can reach up to 8 feet. If you do see one, try to estimate its length. It uses its body to constrict—you guessed it—rodents like rats.

Pantherophis obsoletus >

Eastern gray squirrel

Can you spot this mammal in its camouflage fur, bounding through the trees? See if you can spot one hiding some nuts. Play squirrel tag with your hikemates—hide a few hickory nuts and see if they can find them.

Sciurus carolinensis builds its nest in tree cavities >

3

BIRDWATCH AT CONSTITUTION MARSH

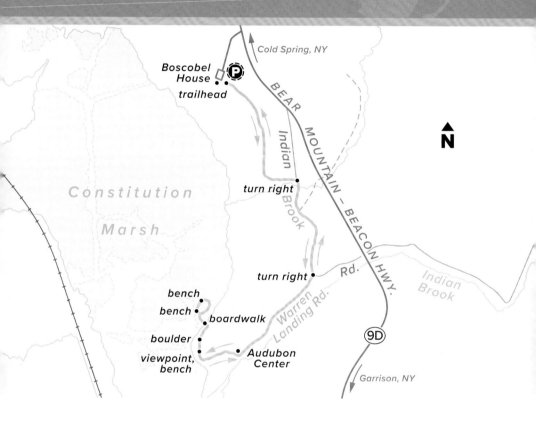

Boscobel House
trailhead

Cold Spring, NY

BEAR MOUNTAIN – BEACON HWY.

Indian Brook

turn right

Constitution

Marsh

turn right Rd.

Indian Brook

bench
bench
boulder

Warren Landing Rd.

boardwalk

9D

viewpoint,
bench

Audubon Center

N

Garrison, NY

YOUR ADVENTURE

Adventurers, let's explore the boardwalks of a tidal marsh on the historical homeland of the Lenape. You're in the Hudson Highlands now, the home of 200 species of birds and 30 species of fish. From the parking lot, follow the green diamonds through the woods and onto Indian Brook Road. Look for the blue diamonds at the intersection with Beverly Warren Road and follow them down toward the visitor center. Cross a wooden bridge over a creek

LENGTH

2.5 miles
out and back

ELEV [FT]

400-

0-

Elevation Gain
164ft.

DISTANCE [MI]

HIKE + EXPLORE 2 hours

DIFFICULTY Moderate—short, but a rocky ascent and descent make it a bit more difficult for youngsters. Hazards may include ticks, inclement weather, stinging insects, poison ivy, and the occasional copperhead or rattlesnake, so please be cautious on your adventure.

SEASON Year-round

GET THERE From Cold Spring, take NY-9D south. Parking for Boscobel House and Gardens will be on your right. Reservations are required to park in the lot (visit bit.ly/timbermarshparking).

Google Maps: bit.ly/timberconstitutionmarsh

RESTROOMS At parking lot

FEE $12 for adults, $6 for children; this also includes admission to the beautiful Boscobel Gardens

TREAT YOURSELF North of the parking area in downtown Cold Spring, Moo Moo's Creamery serves homemade scoops. Our favorite is the maple walnut.

Constitution Marsh, The Audubon Society
(845) 265-2601
Facebook @ConstitutionMarsh
Instagram @ConstitutionMarsh

Step out onto the boardwalk

and continue through the forest. Soon you'll reach a rocky area—hold small hands as you scramble briefly over this part and turn right with the water on your left. It's perfect timing for a power-up rest at a beautiful wooden viewpoint bench. Just a bit farther, past a huge boulder, you'll reach the boardwalk. Step onto Jim's Walk, named after the warden of the sanctuary up until 1998. Trek all the way around the boardwalk, viewing the hills around you and powering up at benches along the way. When you're ready, turn back the way you came and be sure to stop in the visitor center for some cool displays before you leave.

SCAVENGER HUNT

Water chestnut

Look for this invasive species winding around the water and forming mats. Point out the biggest mat you see. Count the triangular, toothed leaves on one mat. Then picture a stem below the mat that goes all the way to the bottom of the marsh, anchoring it. Try sketching it in your nature journal.

< *Trapa natans* (*natans* means "swim" or "float" in Latin)

Seasonal special: American black duck

The marsh is an important migration stopover for many bird species, and the American Black Duck loves to winter here. Where would you winter if you could? Males have a dark brown body and yellow bill

and females have a dull gray bill. Give your best quack out over the water.

Anas rubripes ↗

Seasonal special: tree swallow

Look for this turquoise bird chasing after flying insects above the marsh, doing cool twists and turns. A group of them is known as a stand, and you might just see such a flying stand forming a tornado, getting ready to migrate south as fall approaches.

< *Tachycineta bicolor*

Seasonal special: bald eagle

Winter is a prime time to spot this majestic bird at the marsh; bring your binoculars to get a good look at its hunting behavior. Bald eagles will sometimes snatch a fish right out of another bird's talons. Play "eagle tag" with a hiking buddy and try to steal each other's snacks.

Haliaeetus leucocephalus (*leucocephalus* means "white head" in Latin) ∧

Snapping turtle

This is one of the largest turtles in North America. You might find one in the marsh, but around June, it can also be found on land looking for a place to lay eggs. This reptile is an omnivore, which means it eats both plants and animals. It's also nocturnal, so it would be special to see one in the daytime.

Chelydra serpentina >

4

SEE THE CAVE AT DOVER STONE CHURCH

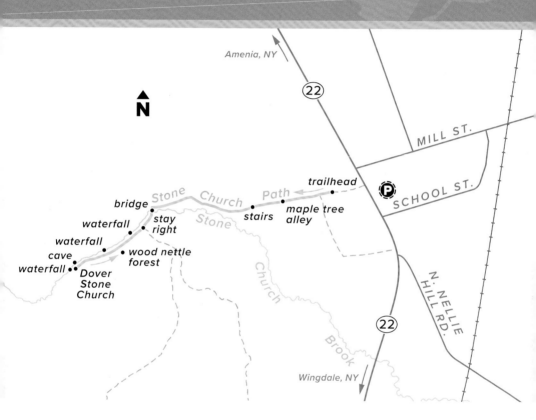

YOUR ADVENTURE

Adventurers, we are headed out on the historical homeland of the Schaghticoke, Mohawk, and Pequot to see a natural curiosity that tourists have been seeking since 1836. You'll start in a maple tree alley—how many can you count as you walk down this pathway? Then you'll climb stairs and find yourself in a Norway maple forest, perhaps stopping at great power-up

LENGTH

1 mile

out and back

ELEV [FT]

700–

300–

Elevation Gain
123ft.

DISTANCE [MI]
1   2   3   4

HIKE + EXPLORE 1 hour

DIFFICULTY Easy—a short, flat excursion. Be careful in the cave as rocks can get slippery.

SEASON Year-round. Fall is best because of the changing leaves. Path and cave can be icy in winter.

GET THERE The trailhead is on the west side of NY-22 at the end of Stone Church Lane, just south of the light at Mill Street. The parking lot at the trailhead is private, but all visitors have permission to park in the school or deli across the street.

Google Maps: bit.ly/timberstonechurch

RESTROOMS None

FEE None

TREAT YOURSELF Just a minute up the road is Kelly's Creamery and Kelly's Husband's Truck, the perfect spot for post-hike rewards.

Dutchess Land Conservancy,
New York-New Jersey Trail Conference
(845) 677-3002 and (201) 512-9348
Facebook @DutchessLandConservancy,
@NJNYTC

The Dover Stone Church cave opening

spots by the creek before heading onward. When you're done powering up, cross the footbridge and keep going until you reach a junction. Head right to the cave. Soon, the 10-mile-long Stone Church Brook is on your right side as you rock-hop your way through the wooden nettle forest. You'll pass two mini waterfalls—what would you name them? Finally, the steeple of rock appears before you. If the water is low, carefully walk on the rocks to explore inside Dover Stone Church and see if you can spot the waterfall inside. Take another power-up stop and head back the way you came.

SCAVENGER HUNT

Stone Church waterfall

Using care and caution, look for the waterfall in the back of the cave. See if you can feel its mica slate rock. This rock is metamorphic, which means it was transformed by heat or pressure. Can you imagine what creatures might drink from the pool at the bottom of the waterfall?

The mini waterfall inside the cave >

Norway maple

Look carefully at the five lobes of the pointed Norway maple leaf. Trace it in your nature journal, and try to match the color when you get home. What name would you give that color? Will the leaves be a different color if you visit at another time of year?

< An alley of *Acer platanoides* in summer and a single leaf sporting fall color

Church from the past

The Stone Church has inspired many artists over the centuries. Former Dover Town Clerk Richard Maher wrote, circa 1907, "Its melodious stream has chanted a requiem over . . . generations dead and gone, And still the ancient arch guards the wild ravine, and the never-tiring stream." Sit for five minutes and try to write a small poem or sketch about how you feel looking at the cave.

< A graphite sketch from 1847 by artist Asher Brown Durand

Small waterfall

Take a power-up at this small waterfall on Stone Church Brook. The creek joins Wells Brook and soon meets with Tenmile River, which flows for 15 miles to the Housatonic River, a 149-mile river that travels all the way to the ocean and drains into Long Island Sound. Everything is connected! Send a leaf boat down the brook, make a wish, and think about whether it could it make it all the way to the ocean. How long do you think it would take?

< Small waterfall on your way to the cave

5

GO ROUND AND ROUND LAKE MINNEWASKA

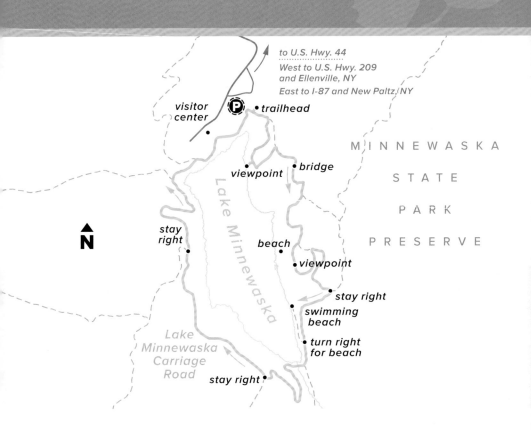

to U.S. Hwy. 44

*West to U.S. Hwy. 209
and Ellenville, NY*

East to I-87 and New Paltz, NY

visitor
center

trailhead

• bridge

viewpoint

MINNEWASKA

STATE

PARK

PRESERVE

*stay
right*

Lake Minnewaska

beach

viewpoint

stay right

swimming
beach

turn right
for beach

Lake
Minnewaska
Carriage
Road

stay right

N

YOUR ADVENTURE

Welcome to a sky lake (clear and fed only by rainwater), adventurer. Your hike around it will be on the historical homeland of the Lenape. You're in the "Gunks," or Shawangunk Mountains, a long ridge that is part of the Appalachian Mountains. Head left from the parking lot, follow the red blazes, and soon you'll reach your first viewpoint of the 33-acre lake. Be careful as you pause for a power-up on the quartz. You'll walk along old carriage roads

LENGTH

2.3-mile

loop

ELEV [FT]

2,000–

1,600–

Elevation Gain

]140ft.

DISTANCE [MI]

1   2   3   4

HIKE + EXPLORE 1.5 hours

DIFFICULTY Moderate—terrain is easy crushed gravel but there are a few up and downs. Make sure to stay on the Red Lake Shore Trail, as there are a few junctions.

SEASON Year-round. Fall is great for hawk watching. Winter is reserved for cross-country skiing; swimming season runs from late June to early September.

GET THERE From Poughkeepsie, head west on Highway 299. Turn right on Main Street (US-44 / NY-55). The well-marked entrance to Minnewaska State Park Preserve will be on your left. Once you pay admission, turn left where the sign says "Lake" and park in the large parking lot.

Google Maps: bit.ly/timberminnewaska

RESTROOMS At parking lot

FEE $10

TREAT YOURSELF About 15 minutes east in New Paltz, The Bakery has custom cookies to bring on your hike or enjoy afterward.

Minnewaska State Park Preserve, Palisades Parks Conservancy

(845) 255-0752 | Facebook @palisadesparks

The view over the lake

from when there were not one, but two resorts on the lake—built in 1879 and 1887, they both burned down in the 1970s and 80s. Head under a bridge, take in another view, and power up on the cliff bench. Soon you'll take a right that leads down to a swimming beach; consider taking a dip. After enjoying the beach, you'll curve around in the forest—stay right for a long stretch, then stay straight to the other end of the lake. You'll end at the visitor center and back at the parking lot. Be aware of bears here. Don't run, just back away slowly if you encounter one. Consider checking out Awosting Falls on your way out of the park. If you stay overnight, explore the area at Sam Pryor Sha-wangunk Campground, 2 miles east.

SCAVENGER HUNT

Long beech fern
Look for this fern that likes to grow in a colony. Its fiddleheads appear in spring and the leaf should have around twelve leaflets, called pinnae, on opposite sides of the stem. How many do you count?

Phegopteris connectilis >

White-tailed deer
You'll find these mammals throughout the year around the lake; watch for the round, pebbly scat on the ground and look closely to see what they eat. If you spot one, check for antlers; only males have them and they fall off every winter and regrow every summer. Find some sticks on the ground and use them to create your own "antlers." Take a selfie!

< A female *Odocoileus virginianus* grazes

Dwarf pitch pine

Find this globally rare evergreen tree on your hike today. While some of its cones are typical, some are serotinous, which means they require fire to open and spread seeds. This is a clever trick the tree uses to regenerate after wildfires.

Pinus rigida (*rigida* means "stiff" in Latin; so-named for its sturdy trunk) >

Quartz rock

This white rock has survived the forces of glaciation and is from the upper Silurian geologic period, 425–440 million years ago. As you take a safe power-up on one of its ledges, look for evidence of glacier movement long ago:

parallel scratches called striations, half-circle gouges called chatter marks, and patches of smooth rock called glacial polish. How many marks from the glacier can you find today?

Can you find the marks of the past? ↗

Seasonal special: Cooper's hawk

Hawk watchers come every fall to see raptors like the Cooper's hawk migrate south for winter. An acronym, "SPASMATIC," is used to identify differ-ent hawks. It comes from the first letters of shape, pattern, actions, size, multiple attributes, and trust in the concept (believe in your ability to identify birds!). Look for Cooper's hawk's short, rounded wings, which help it chase and feed on songbirds.

< *Accipiter cooperii*

6

SUSPEND YOURSELF AT BLACK CREEK PRESERVE

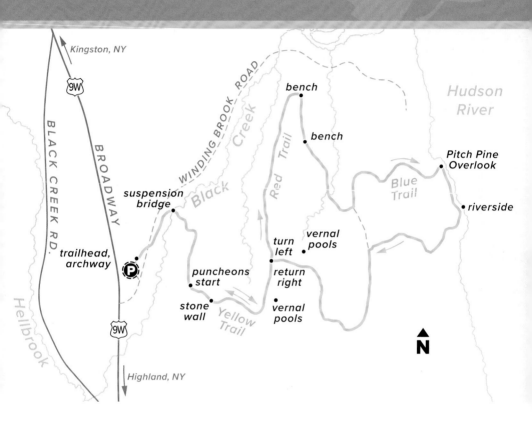

YOUR ADVENTURE

Adventurers, you're on the historical homeland of the Lenape. Walk through the wooden archway, cross a footbridge, and the suspension bridge looms over you. A good picnic power-up awaits below the bridge on the banks of the 46-mile-long Black Creek. This tributary makes it all the way to the Hudson River, whose shoreline you'll soon enjoy. It's black from all the leaves that fall into it. Gradually make your way up the switchbacks.

LENGTH

2.1-mile

lollipop loop

ELEV [FT]

400 –

0

Elevation
Gain

⌐187ft.

1   2   3   4

DISTANCE [MI]

HIKE + EXPLORE 1.5 hours

DIFFICULTY Moderate—on the longer side, with several pushes uphill, but plenty of flat spots

SEASON Year-round. Spring is best for a full creek and budding leaves; winter offers wide-open views of the Hudson; summer is green and shady; fall is bursting with color.

GET THERE South of Kingston on Route 9W, there's a sign on the east side of the highway for Black Creek Preserve. Turn there onto Winding Brook Road and follow to the parking area.

Google Maps: bit.ly/timberblackcreek

RESTROOMS None

FEE None

TREAT YOURSELF 11 minutes south in the town of Highland is Frozen Caboose Ice Cream. Enjoy their huge cones after your hike!

Black Creek Preserve, Scenic Hudson
(845) 473-4440
Facebook @ScenicHudson

Step on up to the suspension bridge, built in 1999

Pass some puncheons (low planks over the swamp) and cross an agricultural stone wall. You'll pass a fern grove, cross a creek on a footbridge, and reach a junction. Turn left on the Red Trail. Look all around you at the ginormous trees and glacial boulders that were lifted and brought here over time. Stay left on the Blue Trail (ignoring a small trail to your right). Finally, you'll reach the Hudson River. Power up, then explore the riverside. Continue on this trail until you connect with the Red Trail, where you will stay left (this time ignoring the small trail to your right) and a short stint of switchbacks will bring you back to the junction with the Yellow Trail—this time, head back toward your car.

SCAVENGER HUNT

Seasonal special: glass eel
In spring, thousands of glass eels (juvenile American eels) arrive at Black Creek. Look for them under rocks in the stream. They've traveled more than 3,000 miles from the Sargasso Sea! They spend up to twenty years here before heading back to the Sargasso to spawn. What's the farthest you've ever traveled?

< The juvenile *Anguilla rostrata*

Hemlock
Can you find the top of a hemlock? It has a little bit of a droop at the top, with feather needles spread out like messy hair. Find its small cones on the ground in fall. Keep one to make your own bird feeder by adding peanut butter and birdseed and hanging it outside.

< Small pine cones of *Tsuga canadensis*

Blueback herring

You are on an important spawning ground for the blueback herring, which journeys from the ocean to deposit its eggs in Black Creek.

Alosa aestivalis >

Pileated woodpecker holes

Sometimes we see the evidence of wildlife before we see the creatures. Look for the holes made by pileated woodpeckers (*Dryocopus pileatus*) in trees, also known as their fast food restaurants. The birds drill into the wood with their beaks, then they use their strong tongues to reach in and grab insects. Do you use your tongue to eat any food in a similar way?

< See if you can spot holes in trees created by red-headed woodpeckers.

Stone wall

Check out this remnant of former enclosures for farm animals. Look closely—can you find an eastern chipmunk hiding in its crevices? Close your eyes and listen for the chipmunk's high-pitched squeak.

< How long do you think this old stone wall is?

1

FIND THE BOULDER NEAR CATSKILL MOUNTAIN HOUSE

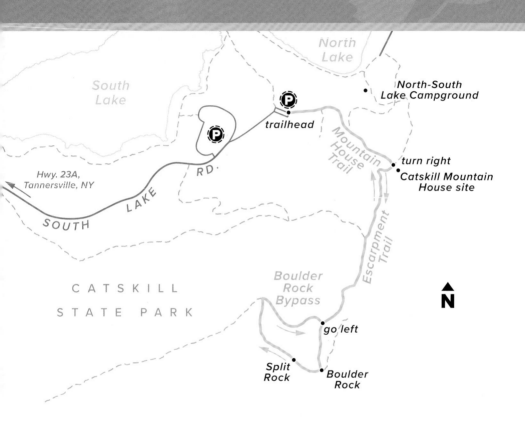

YOUR ADVENTURE

Adventurers, you'll begin this historical and geologic journey on the historical homeland of the Lenape at an unmarked gate. This land is designated as "Forever Wild," which means it can never be developed. The area is called the Catskills after *kaaterskill*, the Dutch term for "big cat creek" and the name early settlers gave nearby Kaaterskill Falls. Follow a long gravel road, passing the first right. Soon, the trail opens up to a beautiful view

LENGTH

1.7-mile

lollipop loop

HIKE + EXPLORE 1.5 hours

DIFFICULTY Moderate—short but rocky with a few climbs. Hand-holding is necessary on steep, exposed ledges.

SEASON Year-round. Winter is great for snowshoeing (park at first lot, adding some distance to your hike).

GET THERE Heading west on NY-23A from Palenville, turn right onto North Lake Road in Haines Falls. Go 2.5 miles, pass Scutt Road and take the next right, before the lake. Follow this for half a mile to the very end. Pass one parking lot and head to the second one. The trailhead is at the gate.

Google Maps: bit.ly/timbercatskill

RESTROOMS At campground (seasonal)

FEE $10

TREAT YOURSELF After hiking, grab lunch or a cup of soup at Selena's Diner, only a few minutes west on NY-23A.

Kaaterskill Wild Forest, New York State Department of Environmental Conservation 518-402-8044 | Facebook @NYSDEC

Judging by its size, Boulder Rock shouldn't be *that* hard to find

and the spot where the Catskill Mountain House once sat. Can you see the Hudson River? On a clear day, you might be looking at five different states! Head past the blue-blazed trailhead into the woods on the right. You pass huge boulders, a couple of ledge views (be careful), and eventually reach a fork. Go left on the red-blazed trail and downhill to reach the huge Boulder Rock. Power up here or on the flat, warm ledge to your left and finish the rest of the loop. Pass Split Rock and a deep crevasse (a large crack in the earth) and arrive back at the first fork. Turn left back toward the Catskill Mountain House site and head back the way you came. Consider camping at North-South Lake Campground when you're done.

SCAVENGER HUNT

Split rock
Glacial erratics are rocks and boulders carried to an area by a glacier then left behind when the ice sheet melts. The glacier that left this split boulder was a mile deep and melted 10,000–12,000 years ago. Imagine the kind of force needed to split this rock or move it anywhere. Try to push it now and see what happens.

< This split rock was left behind by a glacier

Old stone gate
At the start of your adventure, look for two stone columns. These used to be the gateposts for the magnificent Catskill Mountain House, a hotel here in the late 1800s. Can you tell what parts are stone and what parts are old cement?

Remains of the entrance to Catskill Mountain House >

Catskill Mountain House site

Close your eyes and imagine what was once called "America's Grandest Hotel," where three different presidents stayed. Built in 1824, the Catskill Mountain House closed in 1942, was deconstructed, and finally burned to the ground in 1963. In 1826, the *Boston Recorder and Telegraph* wrote that the view

"is indeed magnificent—and he who could look upon such a scene and not turn from it a better man, must truly have forgotten his better elements."

A view of the hotel around 1900 ↗

Quaking aspen

Watch (and hear) the quaking aspen's spade-shaped leaves tremble in the wind. They like to grow in thick stands with all their family nearby. Feel the white bark and look for "aspen eyes" peeking at you from the trunk. Draw the patterns of the bark you see in your nature journal.

Populus tremuloides has a distinctive bark and leaf >

Bracken fern

The first word of bracken fern's scientific name, *Pteridium,* is so named because the fronds look like bird wings—do you agree? Look for this deciduous fern year-round, although it might be yellow or brown when you see it. Feel the front of a pinna (mini leaves across from each other on a stem)—each one is small and rounded. How many do you count?

< *Pteridium aquilinum* is common here

8

ROCK OUT ON THE INDIAN LADDER TRAIL

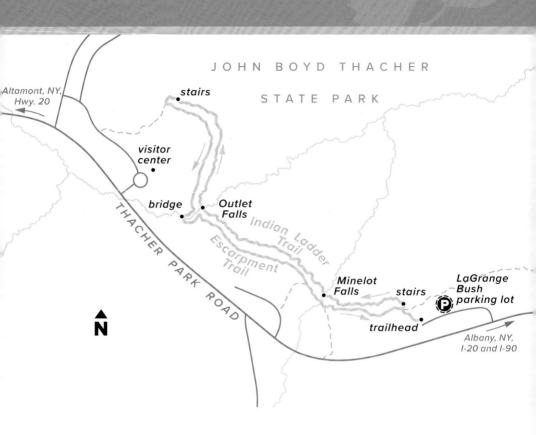

JOHN BOYD THACHER

STATE PARK

Altamont, NY, Hwy. 20

stairs

visitor center

THACHER PARK ROAD

bridge

Outlet Falls

Indian Ladder Trail

Escarpment Trail

Minelot Falls

stairs

LaGrange Bush parking lot

P

trailhead

Albany, NY, I-20 and I-90

N

YOUR ADVENTURE

Adventurers, before you descend the stairs, soak in the view and do a few stretches as you check the horizon for the Adirondacks, Taconics, Berkshires (in Massachusetts), and Greens (in Vermont)—all mountain ranges visible from here in the right conditions. The rock below you is 1100 feet above sea level (and you're heading down part of it) and stretches 10 miles wide on the historical homeland of the Mahican. Head to the right to follow

The view from
Indian Ladder Trail

LENGTH

1-mile loop

HIKE + EXPLORE 1 hour

DIFFICULTY Moderate—short but there are some steep stairs that little ones might need some help with

SEASON Closes during winter months, typically in October with the first frost and opens back up in June or so, based on conditions. Check the website for details.

GET THERE Head northwest on NY-157 W. After you enter John Boyd Thacher State Park, turn right into the LaGrange Bush parking lot.

Google Maps: bit.ly/timberindianladdertrail

RESTROOMS At visitor center

FEE $6

TREAT YOURSELF Try the famous cookies from Bake for You, just 20 minutes east in Slingerlands.

John Boyd Thacher State Park; New York State Parks, Recreation and Historic Preservation
(518) 872-1237
Facebook @ThacherPark
Instagram @ThacherStatePark

this trail counterclockwise from the parking lot and take the stairs downward. Soon you'll reach a small seasonal waterfall on your left; watch for red eft newts here. Cross a bridge, power up under an overhang, and pass a cool fern grotto. Take another two bridges. Can you spot the rock fin that sticks out above you? You'll pass another small cave and cross a bridge over a riverbed, and finally take the stairs back up. Follow the split rail fence overlooking the escarpment and find yourself back at the start. Check out the visitor center when you're done.

SCAVENGER HUNT

Red eft

You can't miss this bright splash of red against the gray backdrop of most rocks, or the green of plants. Red efts sport darker red spots (as many as twenty) outlined in black, as if they were painted on. They love snacking on small invertebrates (animals without backbones)—see if you can spot one munching on a bug or snail.

The red eft is the juvenile eastern newt (*Notophthalmus viridescens*) >

Overhang

This is part of the Helderberg Escarpment, a very rich fossil-bearing formation that dates back to 480 million years ago. Look for the layers of shale, sandstone, and limestone in the rock face. Imagine water seeping through these porous rocks and dissolving them to create caves and overhangs like this one.

Check out the Helderberg Escarpment above you ("clear mountain" in Dutch) >

Bulblet fern

In case you haven't noticed, there are about a gazillion different fern species in the northern mid-Atlantic states. During summer, look underneath the fronds for sori (groups of spores) on the bottom of leaflets.

Cystopteris bulbifera >

Eastern red cedar

Some trees can reproduce with male and female reproductive flowers on the same tree—for the eastern red cedar, they are separated onto different trees. In spring, look for the female trees' small, fleshy, berrylike cones that go on to mature in fall. What happens when you try to smoosh one?

< A hanging branch of *Juniperus virginiana*

Stairs

As you head down the stairs, think of this 1869 quote from author Verplanck Colvin about the Helderberg Escarpment, "It is its romantic wooded rock scenery, dark caverns and sprayey waterfalls, its varied landscape and accessible mountain grandeur that render the Helderberg interesting to artist, author, poet, tourist or rusticator." Sketch what you see in your nature journal.

< Hang on to the railing while you descend

9

ZIG AND ZAG TO THE SUMMIT OF SHELVING ROCK

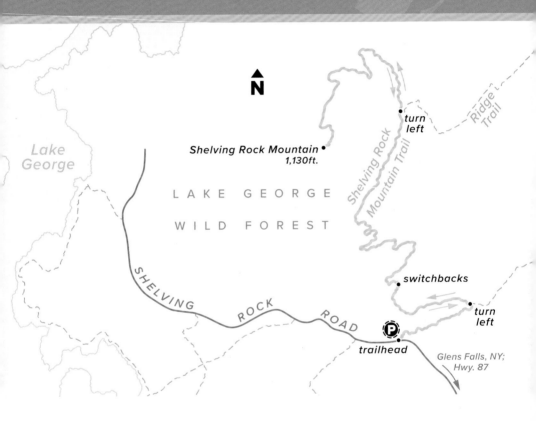

YOUR ADVENTURE

Adventurers, most good things in life take hard work, and this challenging trek is no different. You're on the eastern edge of the 44-square-mile Lake George. You'll be hiking on the historical homeland of the Mohawk, along an old carriage trail of wide and gentle uphills that tycoon George Knapp built to his summer home nearby, circa 1917. Sign the register and start on

LENGTH

3.1 miles

out and back

ELEV [FT]

1,080–

480

1 2 3 4

DISTANCE [MI]

Elevation Gain

595ft.

HIKE + EXPLORE 2 hours

DIFFICULTY Challenging—steady uphill much of the way, but it's a short, low-grade, wide trail

SEASON Year-round

GET THERE From Shelving Rock Road, be sure to go all the way to Parking Lot #4; if you park in the others, you'll have a bit of a walk (though that might be necessary on a busy day). Note: you will be driving on a well-maintained gravel road for a few miles; even a low-clearance car should do fine if you maintain a safe speed.

Google Maps: bit.ly/timbershelvingrock

RESTROOMS None

FEE None

TREAT YOURSELF Fill your bellies with fresh pizza and more at Grumbellies Eatery, just off Highway 4 in Fort Ann. Also, if you keep your eyes peeled, you might luck upon a pie stand in summer along Shelving Rock Road.

Shelving Rock Special Management Area,
Lake George Wild Forest,
New York State Department of
Environmental Conservation
(518) 623-1200
Facebook @NYSDEC

Look down—can you believe a mansion was built just below here?

the gentle incline upward. Watch out for rocks and roots. You'll see a trail sign; turn left and ascend slowly alongside the creek. Soon, the switchbacks begin (trail makers use them so you don't have to climb straight up). Challenge your hiking buddy to count the switchbacks with you and see how many you come up with. Continue zigzagging and look for the seasonal pond to your right. You'll come to another junction; follow the blue blazes left and find your way to the summit. Relax, power up, and head back the way you came. Consider camping on one of the nearby islands to extend the adventure.

SCAVENGER HUNT

Gall

A gall wasp will lay eggs directly into the branch of a tree, and then this ball will grow out from the tree around the larvae. When the gall dries out, the baby wasps make their way through small holes out into the world. Look closely inside. Is there anything left?

Be careful picking up the paper-thin structure >

Hickory

Look for the five alternate (on both sides) leaves of this deciduous tree. The top three are larger than the bottom two or four. Look for hickory nuts on the ground in fall and try to open them. You may not have tasted one before, but they are edible. Sketch the nuts and leaves in your nature journal.

< Carya ovata

Trail register

Registers are a fun way to see who has hiked a trail before you. Flip through and see if you can find someone from a place you've never heard of, then look it up on a map. Don't forget to write in you and your family.

< Sign the register

Lake George Wild Forest

You're in the Adirondacks, and the Lake George Wild Forest is just one of twelve special regions in this mountain range. Named after King George during the French-American War in 1755, Lake George covers 72,508 acres.

Check out the wild forest around you >

Blaze

The NY Department of Environmental Conservation helped blaze this trail. Their mission is "to conserve, improve and protect New York's natural resources and environment and to prevent, abate and control water, land and air pollution, in order to enhance the health, safety and welfare of the people of the state and their overall economic and social well-being." Do you feel healthy and safe outside?

< Can you spot the blue blazes?

10

CAPTURE COBBLE HILL

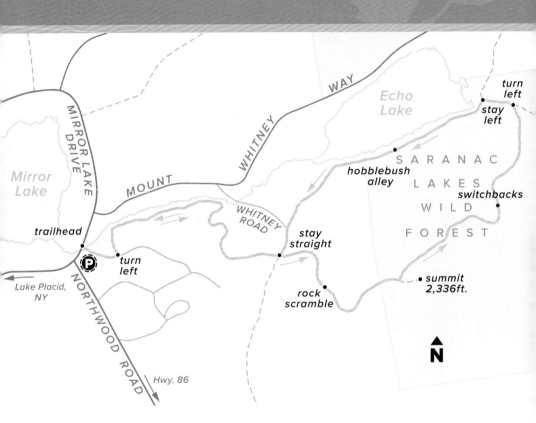

YOUR ADVENTURE

Adventurers, you're going to feel like an Olympian after summiting Cobble Hill in the two-time Olympic host city of Lake Placid. You're hiking today on the historical homeland of the Mohawk. From Mirror Lake Drive, look for trail signs and follow them into the woods. You'll soon come to a trail to your left that will wind its way to your first junction. Stay straight there

LENGTH

2.3-mile

lollipop loop

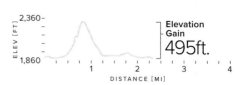

2,360–

ELEV [FT]

1,860

Elevation Gain

495ft.

DISTANCE [MI]

1   2   3   4

HIKE + EXPLORE 1.5 hours

DIFFICULTY Moderate with several pushes uphill and a difficult spot with a rope that could be challenging for your younger hikers; plenty of flat spots. Can be muddy.

SEASON Year-round. Beautiful fall colors. Snowshoes or spikes required in winter.

GET THERE Take NY-86 W 1 mile east of downtown Lake Placid south of Mirror Lake. Turn left onto Northwood Road until you reach Mirror Lake Drive. Parking is available in designated spots along Mirror Lake Drive and in municipal lots. Plans for a new permanent trailhead are being discussed, so check ahead before beginning your journey.

Google Maps: bit.ly/timbercobblehill

RESTROOMS None

FEE None

TREAT YOURSELF Across the lake on Main Street, Emma's Lake Placid Creamery has ice cream of every kind.

Saranac Lakes Wild Forest, NYC Department of Environmental Conservation, Adirondack Land Trust 518-897-1200, (518) 576-2400 Facebook @NYSDEC, @ADKLandTrust Instagram @AdirondackLandTrust

< A helpful rope is on hand for the final summit push

to head uphill (don't worry, it's easy coming down). Scramble over the slick rocks (there's a rope to help you along the way) and keep going, up, up, up, until you reach a trail to the right—this is the summit! After relaxing on the warm rock, enjoying the view, and powering up, you're ready to make your descent on the much gentler path alongside Echo Lake. Head down from the summit and continue to your right. At the next intersection at the edge of the lake, head left along a nice, flat trail surrounded by hobblebushes. Power up one more time when the trees open to a perfect chill spot. Stay left at the next two junctions and then turn right at that original intersection with Whitney Road onto the trail you started in on. Turn right one more time to return to Mirror Lake Drive and your car.

SCAVENGER HUNT

Echo Lake

On the last half of the hike, you'll skirt Echo Lake—notice its calm, flat waters. Take a picture of the reflection or call out and see if an echo comes back to you.

< Can you see your reflection?

Canada mayflower

Look for this plant's white flowers in May and June. Its leaves form a carpet on the forest floor—it spreads using rhizomes, like computer cables running underground. Try drawing what you think things look like underground here in your nature journal.

Maianthemum canadense >

Bunchberry

In spring, look for the four white bracts (petal-like leaves) that surround the bunches of tiny green flowers in the middle. In summer, you'll find bright red berries. The leaves are shiny, large, and in groups of four that turn purple in fall. Lots of animals like to snack on the berries. Challenge yourself to sit still and watch your area for five minutes in silence to see who happens by.

Cornus canadensis >

Sensitive fern

How sensitive are you to cold? Can you take it, or do you get cold quickly? This sensitive fern responds to frost conditions by turning black and dying off quickly for the season. Notice its simple, wiggly leaflets (pinnae) and how different they are from other ferns you've seen.

< *Onoclea sensibilis*

Hobblebush

Look for hobblebush's flat-topped clusters of white flowers in spring and its heart-shaped leaves year-round. If you find a leaf on the ground, make a valentine of it for someone special in your life.

Viburnum lantanoides >

11

CONQUER MOUNT ARAB FIRE TOWER

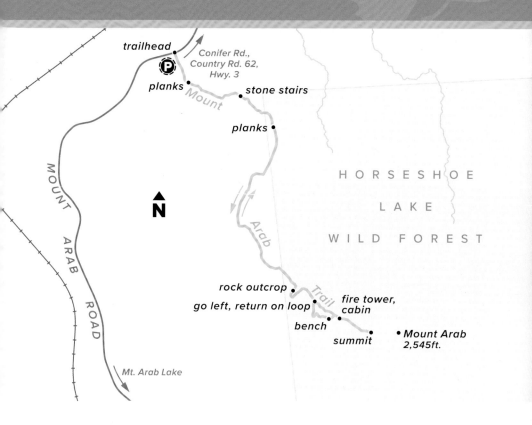

trailhead

Conifer Rd., Country Rd. 62, Hwy. 3

planks

stone stairs

Mount

planks

MOUNT ARAB ROAD

N

Arab

HORSESHOE

LAKE

WILD FOREST

rock outcrop

go left, return on loop

Trail

fire tower, cabin

bench

summit

Mount Arab 2,545ft.

Mt. Arab Lake

YOUR ADVENTURE

Adventurers, welcome to what was originally called Mont Érable by the French (Mount Maple in English), which became Mount Arable, and eventually just Mount Arab, on the historical homeland of the Mohawk. Did you know that if you also scale nearby Coney Mountain and Goodman Mountain, you can earn the Tupper Lake Triad badge? For now, start the trail at a junction—you can choose either direction as both trails connect in

LENGTH

2.1 miles out and back

ELEV [FT]
2,550
1,800

Elevation Gain
727ft.

DISTANCE [MI]
1   2   3   4

HIKE + EXPLORE 2 hours

DIFFICULTY Moderate—a bit on the longer side with several pushes uphill; plenty of flat spots

SEASON Year-round. Best in summer. Popular with snowshoers in winter.

GET THERE At Piercefield, turn south off NY-3 onto County Road 62 / Conifer Road. Turn left onto Mt. Arab Road and follow to the parking lot and trailhead on your right.

Google Maps: bit.ly/timbermtarab

RESTROOMS At summit

FEE None

TREAT YOURSELF Just a few miles east in Tupper Lake is Skyline Ice Cream. Not only can you grab your favorite scoop and a burger but there's also a super-fun giant Adirondack chair to lounge in.

New York State Department of Environmental Conservation, Friends of Mount Arab
(315) 265-3090
Facebook @NYSDEC, @FriendsofMtArab

∧ You're heading up there!

just a few feet. The gradual uphill begins as you cross a plank and both stone and wooden steps. See if you can count them all. When you reach the huge rock outcropping, you know you're close. At the next junction, go left to take your summit loop clockwise. Come across the tower and the observer's cabin and give it a climb. How many steps do you take on the way up? Be careful and hang on to the rails. Enjoy the view of the Horseshoe Lake Wild Forest and take a deep breath. When you're done powering up, head down the other trail near the tower to discover two secret bench viewpoints—perfect for a snack. Consider staying the night near Tupper Lake.

SCAVENGER HUNT

Tower

Imagine this tower being constructed of wood in the early
1900s! It was rebuilt in 1918 using
steel. What do you think the main
differences between wood and
steel would be for construction?
There once were fifty-seven steel
fire towers; only thirty-five are

left. Enjoy this one while you can. The inside is only open in summer.

Your reward for the climb: a room with a view ↗

Observer's cabin

First built in 1912 and then rebuilt in the 1950s, this cabin hosted fire observers for seventy years. Can you spot Mount Arab Lake and Eagle Crag Lake to the west? How about Tupper Lake, Mount Morris, and the High Peaks? Use the compass app on your smartphone to look around.

< View from atop the tower

Red trillium

Look for these three ovate (rounded) leaves any time of year, and in spring, look for a beautiful flower with three red petals. Can you see where *tri*-llium gets its name? After a few weeks, the petals wither to leave behind a small fruit. Take a whiff—its smell is *not* appealing, but it helps to attract a specific fly for pollination.

Trillium erectum >

Wood sorrel

This is a shade-tolerant plant, which means it can survive without much sunlight. Look for it carpeting the forest floor during your hike and trace its clover-like leaves in your nature journal.

< Spot *Oxalis* by its leaves that look like clover

Mount Arab Lake

From the bench, you can see Mount Arab Lake and Eagle Crag Lake. On the other side is Tupper Lake, named after Ansel Tupper, a land surveyor. It is 41 miles long and fed by the 146-mile-long Raquette River.

Have a seat and take in the view >

12

FEEL THE RUSH AT STONE VALLEY

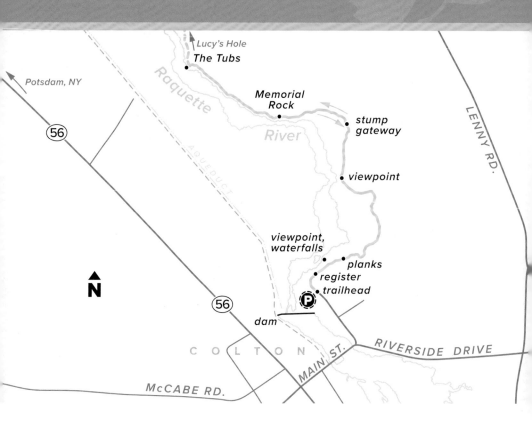

Lucy's Hole
The Tubs

Potsdam, NY

Raquette

56

River

AQUEDUCT

Memorial
Rock

stump
gateway

viewpoint

viewpoint,
waterfalls

planks

register

trailhead

56

dam

LENNY RD.

C O L T O N

MAIN ST.

RIVERSIDE DRIVE

McCABE RD.

N

YOUR ADVENTURE

Adventurers, you're about to feel the power of nature on the historical homeland of the Mohawk. Start out under the big wooden arch and follow a bed of pine needles. There aren't many blazes on this trail, but just keep the river on your left and you'll be fine. You'll hear the *whoosh* of the 146-mile-long Raquette River beside you—don't worry, you'll get to see it soon! Sign

LENGTH

1.8 miles

out and back

Elevation Gain
131ft.

HIKE + EXPLORE 1.5 hours

DIFFICULTY Moderate—nice and short, but a few ups and downs, rocks and roots. There are also sections of exposed ledges, so don't be afraid to hold hands.

SEASON Year-round. Best spring through early fall and for snowshoeing in winter.

GET THERE Heading on NY-56 S through Colton, turn left onto Main Street, cross the Raquette River, and take a left onto Riverside Drive. The parking lot is at the end of the road by the river.

Google Maps: bit.ly/stonevalleytrail

RESTROOMS None

FEE None

TREAT YOURSELF Yum Yum's Chilly Delight offers DIY frozen yogurt just 15 minutes north in Potsdam.

Stone Valley Cooperative Recreation Area, Laurentian Chapter Adirondack Mountain Club
(315) 262-2571
Facebook @adkmtnclub

Power up here along the Raquette River

the register and look at the folks who have come before you from other places. Who traveled the farthest? Your first side trail to the left leads to a viewpoint of the first falls. Be careful—this is a dam and the water fluctuates unexpectedly, so view from afar. Back on the main trail, cross some planks and carefully check out the rocky viewpoint. On the main trail, walk through two sentinel stumps guarding a tree and find a large boulder with a memorial plaque. Keep going and you'll reach your adventure's final highlight—the Tubs waterfall! Head back the way you came. (Or, if your squad is looking for more adventure, it's just another hour on the Stone Valley Trail to Lucy's Hole—another rock outcrop and river drop.)

SCAVENGER HUNT

Plaque honoring Lew Weeks
Beautiful lands don't just take care of themselves. They are the result of hard work by people like you who put effort into taking care of our trails for generations to come. Give a high five to this plaque and thank Lew Weeks for his important and appreciated support of this trail!

< Find this commemorative plaque on your hike

Royal fern
Hello, Your Majesty! This is called royal fern because of its size. Put your hand up to one of its pinnae (leaflets)—are your fingers smaller or bigger? The genus name *Osmunda* comes from "Osmunder," a Saxon name for the god Thor. Legend has it he hid his family in a clump of royal fern to protect them.

Osmunda regalis var. *spectabilis* >

Hemlock bark

Look across the river as you begin your trail. The ruins you see are of a former tannery, which turned hides into leather using the bark of the hemlock trees so common here. Bark was stripped, dried, shredded, and placed in tubs of hot water to leach out tannins that were then used in making leather. See if you can identify a hemlock by its bark.

< Hemlock bark was used for tanning hides

American beech

Look on the ground for this ovate (rounded) leaf with toothed edges. This is a deciduous tree, so the leaves will turn yellow and drop in fall. See the exposed beech tree roots behind the leaf in the photo? This tree likely grew on a nurse log, which later rotted away, leaving the roots exposed. Can you find another tree with aboveground roots?

< Leaf of *Fagus grandifolia*

Potholes at the Tubs

Take a minute to watch the water and how it flows over this rock. In spring, the water flows and pushes around smaller stones, which grind into the rock, creating more potholes. Imagine how much water came through here 12,000–14,000 years ago when glaciers were melting. Nowadays, the dam controls the water.

How old do you think these holes are? >

13

SCALE THE SPINE OF BALD MOUNTAIN TO THE FIRE TOWER

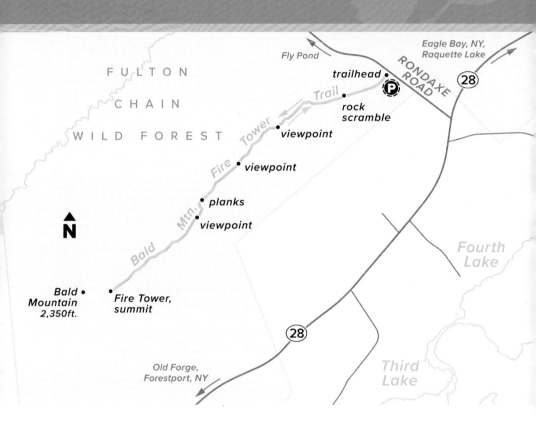

Eagle Bay, NY, Raquette Lake

Fly Pond

trailhead

RONDAXE ROAD

28

FULTON

CHAIN

WILD FOREST

Trail

rock scramble

viewpoint

Fire Tower

viewpoint

planks

viewpoint

Bald Mtn.

N

Fourth Lake

Bald Mountain 2,350ft.

Fire Tower, summit

28

Old Forge, Forestport, NY

Third Lake

YOUR ADVENTURE

Adventurers, welcome to Bald Mountain Tower, on the historical home-land of the Mohawk in the Adirondack Mountains. This is also known as Rondaxe Mountain (created from the word "Adirondacks") to differentiate it from other nearby Bald Mountains. This was one of 120 fire towers (like Mount Arab's) constructed in the early 1900s to report smoke sightings to

LENGTH

2 miles out and back

Elevation Gain

376ft.

HIKE + EXPLORE 1 hour

DIFFICULTY Moderate—short, but a fair amount of climbing on unusual, rocky terrain. You'll want to keep little ones close, as there are abrupt drop-offs.

SEASON Year-round. Incredible fall foliage. Spring can be muddy and spikes or snowshoes are recommended in winter.

GET THERE Take NY-28 about 30 miles north of Forestport. Turn left onto Rondaxe Road and the parking lot is a little ways down on your left.

Google Maps: bit.ly/timberrondaxe

RESTROOMS At trailhead (mid-May to November)

FEE None

TREAT YOURSELF At the Pied Piper in Old Forge you can grab a big waffle cone and rest your legs on the grassy shores of Old Forge Pond.

Fulton Chain Wild Forest, New York State Department of Environmental Conservation (315) 866-6330 | Facebook @NYSDEC

∧ **Ready to climb Bald Mountain Tower?**

forest rangers. Observers also used it to record where planes flew during World War II. Sign the register and walk through the rooty woods until they open up onto the ridgeline—a flat stone outcropping you can hop up on like a mountain goat. There will be a light rock scramble on a red-blazed trail— littles should be careful. Head up the rock face, finding roots to help you up, until you see a rocky viewpoint; power up here. Hike back up the spine, where you'll see planks and one more rocky view—then it really opens up. The only thing between you and the fire tower is a bunch of slick rock! Carefully approach the staircase and step your way up, taking in the view at the top. Return the way you came, carefully making your way down the rocky path.

SCAVENGER HUNT

Fire tower

At more than 2,000 feet elevation, the view from atop the fire tower stretches many miles if the weather cooperates. Sketch what you can see in your nature journal. Like the Mount Arab fire tower, this lookout was first built of wood, then replaced by steel in 1917.

< **View from the Bald Mountain (Rondaxe) fire tower**

Quartz vein

The metamorphic (transformed by heat or pressure) rock of Bald Mountain dates back to Precambrian time and is 900 to 1600 million years old. How long would it take you to count to 900 million?

Vein of quartz in metamorphic rock >

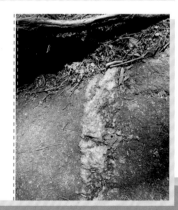

American mountain ash

Check out the leaves of this tree. They are pinnate, which means they come out on both sides of the stem, directly opposite each other. They turn orange in fall. Notice the bright red stems. White flowers in spring are followed by bright red berries in summer. Trace the leaves in your nature journal.

< *Sorbus americana*

Old man's beard lichen

This isn't a plant—but what is it? It is lichen, a combination of algae and fungi; there are over 800 types in New York! Keep your eyes peeled for different types as you hike. This kind is "fruticose," or branched. If you find a loose clump, hold it up to your chin and take a selfie with your new "beard."

< Can you find a clump of lichen?

View of the lakes

From the fire tower, can you see the Fulton Chain of Lakes below? How many do you see? They are named First, Second, Third, and so on—there are eight altogether. The dammed Moose River creates the chain of lakes, and it holds back almost 7 billion gallons of water!

Lakes as far as the eye can see >

14

BOARDWALK YOURSELF AROUND BEAVER LAKE

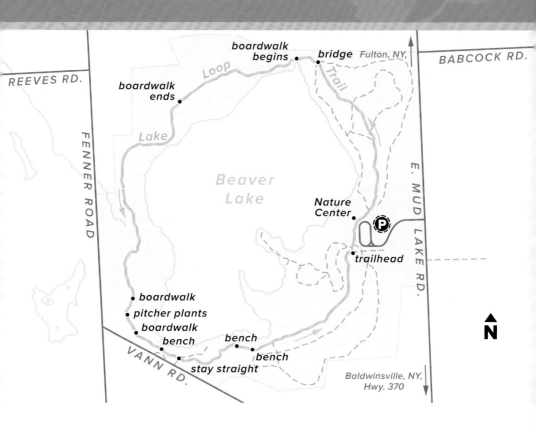

REEVES RD.

FENNER ROAD

Loop

boardwalk begins

boardwalk ends

Lake

Beaver Lake

bridge *Fulton, NY,*

BABCOCK RD.

Trail

Nature Center

E. MUD LAKE RD.

trailhead

boardwalk

pitcher plants

boardwalk

bench

bench

bench

stay straight

VANN RD.

Baldwinsville, NY, Hwy. 370

N

YOUR ADVENTURE

Adventurers, welcome to the historical homeland of the Onondaga. You'll be circumnavigating (going all the way around) beautiful Beaver Lake, encountering some of its more than 200 species of birds and 800 varieties of plants. From the parking lot, find the sign for Lake Loop Trail and head counterclockwise. You'll have the cushy padding of needles and bark most

LENGTH

2.8-mile loop

Elevation Gain 60ft.

ELEV [FT] 700– 300

DISTANCE [MI] 1 2 3 4

HIKE + EXPLORE 2 hours

DIFFICULTY Easy—longer than some adventures, but trail is level and wide; perfect for letting your littles run ahead and gain independence

SEASON Year-round. Fall has great colors and migrating birds; spring is when everything comes back to life; and summer is lush, cool, and breezy. Winter is open for cross-country skiing only.

GET THERE Take NY-370 west from Baldwinsville, turn north onto E Mud Lake Road, and the Beaver Lake Nature Center will be on your left.

Google Maps: bit.ly/timberbeaver

RESTROOMS At Nature Center

FEE $5, payable when you leave

TREAT YOURSELF Emmi's Farm Market, just 5 minutes away on W Genesee Road, has fresh strawberries and more.

Onondaga County Parks, Beaver Lake Nature Center
(315) 638-2519
Facebook @OnondagaCountyParks,
@BeaverLakeNatureCenter

∧ One of many boardwalk sections around Beaver Lake, which allow you to spot plants and creatures from above

of the way around. Begin at the sensory garden and frog pond; you'll cross the yellow Woodland Trail and purple Deep Woods Trail, but just stay straight on the Lake Loop path. You'll cross a bridge and soon the boardwalk begins. Take a power-up with a view on the bench, cross another bridge and reach another boardwalk zone, including the fern alley. See how many different kinds of ferns you can spot. Take another power-up on a bench, pass the cabbage swamp, take in another view, cross a bridge, and admire the triple-trunk tree. You'll head into the forest after your last boardwalk. Pass a trail crossing and go straight. Make your way to the end of the loop and the parking lot.

SCAVENGER HUNT

Green arrow arum

The arrow marks the spot! Feel this plant's large leaf blade and trace it in your nature journal. What kind of creatures can you make from its shape? Add eyes, mouth, and legs and see what happens.

Peltandra virginica >

Tulip tree

While its common name comes from its tulip-like blooms, this deciduous tree's wide leaves also resemble tulip blooms. Look for its leaves to turn yellow and drop in fall and make your own "tulip" bouquet.

Liriodendron tulipifera >

Midland painted turtle

Do you like to bask in the sun? Keep an eye out for New York's most common turtle. Look for its bright stripes of yellow and red on its neck and shell. Try to watch its behavior and sketch it in your nature journal.

Chrysemys picta marginata hanging out on a log >

White oak

Feel the seven to nine rounded lobes on the leaves of this deciduous tree. In fall, its leaves turn red and drop. In spring, look for its droopy male catkins and red female flowers, both on the same tree.

< The leaf of *Quercus alba*

Pitcher plant

Look deep into the mouth of this carnivorous (animal-eating) plant. Its brightly colored veins are designed to lure in prey. When an insect comes close to explore, it often falls into the liquid held inside and gets digested. If you were a plant, how might you lure insects to come close?

Sarracenia purpurea:
a plant that eats meat! >

15

BRING YOUR FLOCK TO THE AUBURN TRAIL

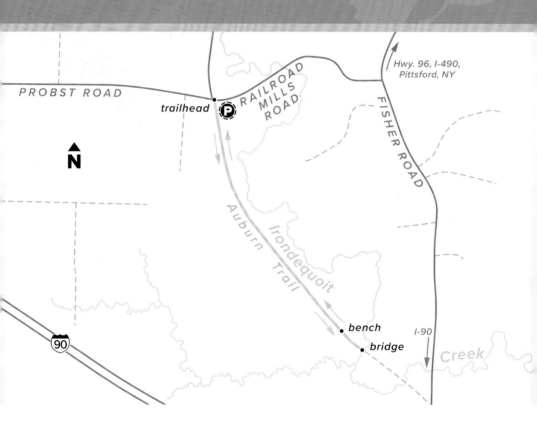

YOUR ADVENTURE

Adventurers, you're about to walk through a bird neighborhood bustling with activity! Wildlife watching takes patience and a keen eye and ear—let's practice those today. We'll be walking along the bed of an old railroad from the mid-1800s on the historical homeland of the Seneca. As you walk, consider that you're in an area that was dominated by glaciers and ice sheets 12,000 years ago. They created a special soil that's perfect for a variety of

LENGTH

1.4 miles

out and back

Elevation Gain
35ft.

HIKE + EXPLORE 1 hour

DIFFICULTY Easy—short and flat

SEASON Year-round. Spring and fall abound with migrating birds.

GET THERE From I-490 E take exit 28 to merge onto NY-96, turn left onto Fisher Road for 1.4 miles, then right on Railroad Mills Road for half a mile until it intersects with Probst Road. The small parking lot will be at the intersection on your left.

Google Maps: bit.ly/timberauburn

RESTROOMS None

FEE None

TREAT YOURSELF Abbott's Frozen Custard in Pittsford offers yummy post-hike cones, floats, and shakes.

Town of Victor Parks and
Recreation Department
585-742-0141
Facebook @VictorPksandRec

You'll be walking to this bridge and back today

plants, and those plants attract a lot of birds. Over 120 species of birds are known to pass through or live in this region! You'll be walking alongside the 4.6-mile-long Irondequoit Creek. Walk slowly and savor all the sights around you. On the left and right, you'll see little bird hotels in the brush. Stand near a hole in a shrub and listen carefully—what do you hear? Once you reach the bridge crossing, take a power-up as you look for bird species you haven't seen yet. Finally, head back the way you came.

SCAVENGER HUNT

Flowering dogwood

Dogwood trees line your trail today. In spring, look for their white flowers; in fall, red berries appear. Actually, what we think of as dogwood flower petals are in fact special leaves called bracts that can be white, pink, or even red. The true flowers are yellowish and in a tiny clump in the center of the bracts. Can you think of another example in nature where something isn't what it seems?

< *Cornus florida*

Monarch butterfly

Monarchs are a type of Lepidoptera, which is an order of insects that are caterpillars as larvae and have four broad wings as adults. The bright orange of their wings is a warning sign to predators: the milkweed plant monarchs eat makes them toxic to creatures who might want to eat them. What other warning signs does nature use?

< *Danaus plexippus*

Purple crown vetch

Each cluster of flowers on this low-growing vine can have up to twenty-five small, roundish parts. Have everybody in your group find a cluster, count the parts, and compare your results.

Securigera varia >

Multiflora rose

Look for this thorny, bushy shrub with toothy oval leaves year-round. In spring, you'll find five-petaled white flowers. It is considered an invasive species, which means it grows really fast and crowds out other plants. In late summer, red seed hips come out, which are rich in vitamin C and sometimes used as a food supplement.

< *Rosa multiflora*

Baltimore oriole

This orange-and-black songbird has a long, pointy beak. You also might hear its whistling song. Can you whistle? How loud? Try sending a whistling call for an oriole. The "Baltimore" part of its common name comes from England's Baltimore family, who have orange and black in their family crest.

A male *Icterus galbula* with a meal in his beak >

16

WIND DOWN AT THE NIAGARA WHIRLPOOL

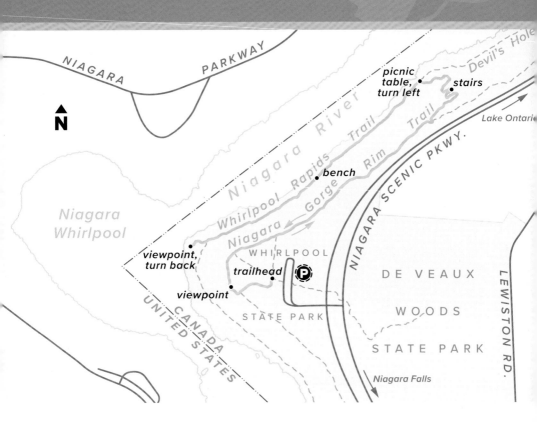

N

NIAGARA   PARKWAY

picnic table, turn left

stairs

Devil's Hole

Lake Ontario

Niagara River

Whirlpool Rapids Trail

Gorge Rim Trail

NIAGARA SCENIC PKWY.

bench

Niagara Whirlpool

Niagara WHIRLPOOL

viewpoint, turn back

trailhead

P

viewpoint

DE VEAUX

WOODS

LEWISTON RD.

CANADA / UNITED STATES

STATE PARK

STATE PARK

Niagara Falls

YOUR ADVENTURE

Adventurers, welcome to the Niagara Gorge, historical homeland of the Haudenosaunee. You're going to walk from the top of the gorge to the bottom to see the famous Niagara Whirlpool, a confluence in the middle of the 38-mile-long Niagara River. Likely named after the Iroquois word "Onguiaahra," which means strait (a narrow passage of water connecting two large bodies of water—in this case, Lake Erie and Lake Ontario), this

LENGTH

2.4 miles out and back

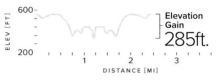

Elevation Gain
285ft.

HIKE + EXPLORE 2 hours

DIFFICULTY Moderate—a bit rocky and there are steps on the way down

SEASON Spring to fall; risk of falling rocks in winter. Best in summer.

GET THERE From Main Street in Niagara Falls, continue north on Lewiston Road and turn left on Findlay Drive until it merges with Niagara Scenic Parkway. Turn left at the sign for Whirlpool State Park.

Google Maps: bit.ly/timberwhirlpool

RESTROOMS At parking lot; open in spring and summer

FEE None

TREAT YOURSELF Hmm . . . donuts or pizza? Yes, definitely. At Frankie's just down the street on Portage Road.

Whirlpool State Park; New York State Parks, Recreation and Historic Preservation
(716) 284-4691
Facebook @NYStateParks

∧ **The cable car heads out over the whirlpool**

section of water is indeed more of a strait than a river. From the parking lot, walk straight ahead to the viewpoint and railing—the water below is where you're headed! Turn right and follow the ridge until you reach the staircase. Turn left and head down the big, stone stairs. How many can you count? Take a power-up stop on the bench at the bottom, then turn left. Walk a bit more and see if you can find a mini whirlpool on the right. Take in a viewpoint, then conquer three sets of rocky steps—carefully. Keep going; you'll soon encounter a small trail through the rocks on the right. Turn here and carefully head out to a flat rock to view the Niagara Whirlpool. Power up here and head back the way you came.

SCAVENGER HUNT

Whirlpool

Look closely. Can you tell that the water is circulating counterclockwise? What are some other whirlpools you have seen? This one is 125 feet deep; what do you think it looks like at the bottom? The whirlpool is controlled by the hydroelectric power plants on the river—when the sun sets, the flow goes down 50 percent and moves clockwise again.

∧ What does the water falling into the whirlpool sound like to you?

Viper's bugloss

See if you can find the non-native viper's bugloss plant. (Hint: "bugloss" is Greek for "tongue.") In early summer, can you spot its vibrant purple flowers? Look closely—the pollen is blue but the filaments (long tongues) are red. How many filaments can you count?

Echium vulgare >

Purple-flowering raspberry

Try a game of "I notice . . . ," "I wonder . . . ," or "It reminds me of . . ." with this five-lobed, maple-like leaf. If the plant is blooming, count the papery petals of the flower and look closely at the small yellow stamen (the fertilizing part) and anthers (pollen). Droopy red berries will replace the blooms in late summer.

< *Rubus odoratus* ("odoratus" means "perfumed" in Latin)

Rock

There are rocks of all sizes and shapes on this adventure. Around 4,500 years ago, the Niagara River eroded the gorge, and that unearthed *another* old gorge called St. David's Gorge, which made the whirlpool. These rocks are the remnants of thousands of years of erosion. How do you think water erodes rock?

How many different rock shapes can you find? >

Blue jay

In Latin, "cristata" means "crested"—can you see the tuft on the blue jay's head? If you find a feather on the ground, look closely. The feathers are actually *not* blue; they have little mirrors on them that refract the color blue back to you. Crazy!

Cyanocitta cristata >

17

SEE AN OLD FLAME IN A WATER-FALL AT ETERNAL FLAME FALLS

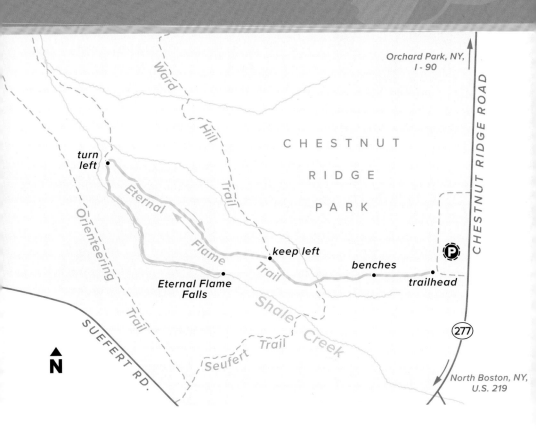

YOUR ADVENTURE

Adventurers, are you ready to gaze into a flame that stays lit, even behind a waterfall? You're on the historical homeland of the Seneca, and you'll kick off straight into the woods. Follow the flame trail markers on the trees as you head down gradually, walking along a wide dirt path surrounded by roots, with trees all around. Finally, when you reach Shale Creek, turn left.

∧ Gazing into the eternal flame is mesmerizing

LENGTH

1.2 miles out and back

ELEV [FT]
1,400 –
1,000 –

Elevation Gain
140ft.

DISTANCE [MI]   1   2   3   4

HIKE + EXPLORE 1 hour

DIFFICULTY Moderate—short with a few roots to negotiate; riverbed can get slippery

SEASON Year-round. Best in late spring. The trail can get slippery after rain, snow, or ice, but the waterfalls will have a bigger flow. Be sure to have your lead hiker bring a lighter in case the flame has gone out.

GET THERE Take N Buffalo Street south from Orchard Park until it becomes NY-277 / Chestnut Ridge Road. Stay straight for 3.3 miles and turn right into the Eternal Flame parking lot in Chestnut Ridge Park.

Google Maps: bit.ly/timbereternal

RESTROOMS None at trailhead, but one can be found at the park's main entrance up the road

FEE None

TREAT YOURSELF Try one of over 100 milkshake flavors and a hot dog at Taffy's, just 6.5 miles north up NY-277.

Erie County Parks, Recreation, and Forestry
(716) 858-8355 | Facebook @ErieCountyParks

At that point, you'll be walking directly up the ravine on a small trail. Walk with care—it can be slippery—and be sure to stay on the trail. Just a bit farther, the waterfall, its grotto behind the falls, and the magically burning flame are revealed.

SCAVENGER HUNT

Eternal Flame Falls

Can you smell rotten eggs? That's natural gas—the eternal flame is fueled by a rupture in the earth that continually releases the gas and keeps the flame lit. (Hiking leads, be sure to bring a lighter, just in case the flame has gone out.) It's believed to have been first lit thousands of years ago by Native Americans.

< 35-foot Eternal Flame Falls

Wood fern

Look for evergreen wood ferns lining the rocks near the eternal flame. The leaves (pinnae) are delicate and lacy, with intricate patterns. They are divided three times into leaflets: large, medium, and small. Try to identify each one.

Dryopteris >

Roots

You'll walk over a lot of roots on your way to the eternal flame. Ponder the function of roots—what are they "rooting for" as they grow down and around? Can you find the end of an exposed root?

Find a tree with exposed roots and try to follow the path of each one >

Shale

This shale is between 416 million and 359 million years old. It has withstood intense pressure over time. Sometimes there were thick pieces of ice on top of it—one ice sheet would melt and another sheet of ice would come and cover it. Each time, the ice broke the rock below, like a break on a frozen lake. One of those fractures released the natural gas that feeds the eternal flame.

< The rock around the flame is shale, sedimentary rock easily split into slabs

Northern red oak

See if you can spot the fastest-growing and largest of all oak tree species in New York, the northern red oak. Its leaves usually have seven to eleven deep lobes. Make a wish if you happen to find a fallen pair of connected acorns—they're considered good luck.

< *Quercus rubra*

18

SOAK UP THE WATERFALLS AT WATKINS GLEN

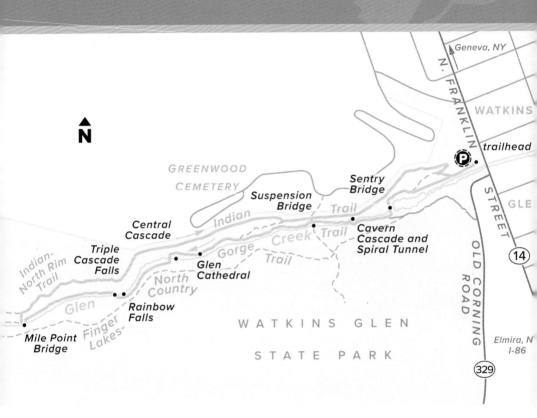

YOUR ADVENTURE

Adventurers, you are standing on the site of a grist mill that opened in the 1800s. The area was opened to tourists in 1863, after which a hotel was built in 1873 and suspension bridge in 1874. Start at the entrance tunnel and begin following Glen Creek, which originates in the hills 7 miles to the west then drops 400 feet as it descends through the park, creating a series of beautiful waterfalls along the way on the historical homeland of the Seneca.

LENGTH

2.3-mile loop

Elevation Gain **433ft.**

HIKE + EXPLORE 1.5 hours

DIFFICULTY Moderate—there are handrails and half of the trail is covered in stone; slow, gentle downgrade on a wide trail back

SEASON The Gorge Trail is closed in winter. Spring has strong waterfall flow and fewer crowds; summer can be hot and crowded; fall has incredible colors.

GET THERE Take NY-14 / N Franklin Street through the town of Watkins Glen and, at Tenth Street, turn into the Watkins Glen State Park entrance and parking lot.

Google Maps: bit.ly/timberwatkins

RESTROOMS At gift shop

FEE $10 per car

TREAT YOURSELF Walk two blocks south to the Great Escape Ice Cream Parlor for a Clown Head, Upside Down Banana Split, or Ice Cream Taco.

Watkins Glen State Park; New York State Parks, Recreation and Historic Preservation
(607) 535-4511 | Facebook @NYStateParks

∧ Welcome to a waterfall lover's nirvana

After it exits, the creek continues and finally ends in nearby Seneca Lake, the deepest of the Finger Lakes. Cross the Sentry Bridge and enter "Glen Alpha," the name bestowed on the first interior section of the gorge in the resort's early days. Walk up the stairs to a beautiful stone arch bridge and the 60-foot-long Central Cascade waterfall. Stop for a power-up here and feel the breeze. Keep walking past Glen Cathedral and see Rainbow Falls and Triple Cascade Falls before continuing on to spectacular Mile Point Bridge. Turn right there to reach an intersection with the Indian / North Rim Trail, a former Seneca tribe hunting trail. Turn right and head down the wide dirt path with the gorge on your right. Or, if you have more energy, you can continue on the upper end of the Gorge Trail to Jacob's Ladder (making a 3-mile round trip hike). Consider extending the fun at nearby Six Nations Campground.

SCAVENGER HUNT

Cavern Cascade

Did you know there are different kinds of waterfalls? Look carefully at each one and see how they are different. This is a single-drop waterfall, where it falls almost vertically and leaves the rock completely.

< You can walk behind this waterfall!

Spiral gorge

The gorge gets narrow here—Pluto Falls is at the top. The light on the layers of rock is good for the imagination. What can you envision in the stone patterns and shadows?

Here the gorge zigs and zags >

Central Cascade

The highest waterfall in the park, the Central Cascade, is spectacular. A Civilian Conservation Corps crew used natural stone to create the bridge and stairs around you. Can you imagine a major flood washing through here? One did in 1935, sending massive amounts of water down the gorge and forcing reconstruction of the trails.

< The Central Cascade waterfall is 60 feet high

Rainbow Falls

This waterfall drops into a pothole pool—how do you think the pool was created over time? If you are at this spot in the afternoon, the sun rays might fall through the canyon and create a rainbow. See if you can capture it with your camera—without getting yourself or the camera wet!

< Can you spot the rainbow?

Seasonal special: gray petaltail

This gorge is a special place—one of only eleven confirmed locations where you can find this rare species of dragonfly. This is a protected species, so if you see one flying around be sure to treat it with the respect and care it deserves. Let a park ranger know about your sighting.

Tachopteryx thoreyi >

19

TAKE IT IN AT TAUGHANNOCK FALLS

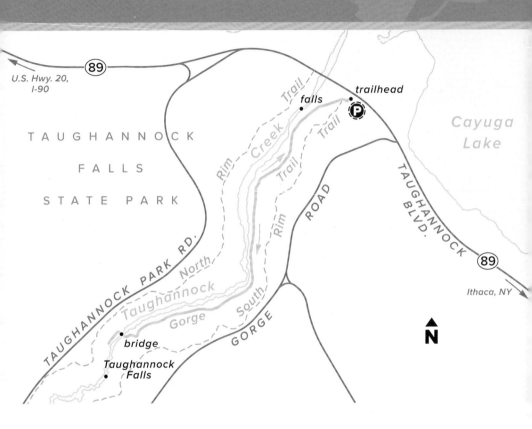

US. Hwy. 20, I-90

89

TAUGHANNOCK FALLS STATE PARK

Rim

Creek

Trail

Trail

Trail

falls

trailhead

Cayuga Lake

ROAD

Rim

TAUGHANNOCK BLVD.

89

Ithaca, NY

TAUGHANNOCK PARK RD.

North

Taughannock

Gorge

South

GORGE

bridge

Taughannock Falls

N

YOUR ADVENTURE

Adventurers, ready for the show? You'll feel like you're at the movies as you approach this waterfall on the historical homeland of the Cayuga Nation. Taughannock Falls drops 215 feet in this beautiful amphitheater of rock, making it the tallest free-falling waterfall east of the Mississippi River. Start at the first falls (not the main attraction) and take a pre-power-up

∧ Taughannock Falls is named after the Algonquin word for "in the trees"

LENGTH

2 miles out and back

ELEVATION GAIN
75ft.

HIKE + EXPLORE 1 hour

DIFFICULTY Easy—flat, wide, short trail with gravel

SEASON Year-round. If conditions are icy, the overlook and parts of the trail might be closed, so be sure to call ahead. Spring offers beautiful wildflowers.

GET THERE Head north from Ithaca on NY-89 and turn left into the Taughannock Falls State Park parking lot.

Google Maps: bit.ly/timbertaughannock

RESTROOMS At park office across the street from parking lot

FEE $9 per vehicle

TREAT YOURSELF Purity Ice Cream Company in Ithaca has sweets, treats, and homemade eggnog in fall.

Taughannock Falls State Park; New York State Parks, Recreation and Historic Preservation

(607) 387-6739 | Facebook @NYSDEC

on one of the benches. Then head out on the wide, flat trail as you walk past a large embankment on your left and the creek to your right. Check out the trees leaning toward the edge like they're going to fall—what do you think causes that? Be sure to check out the potholes—carefully. The trail then passes under a canopy of trees, and there are some perfectly flat rocks you can sit on to power up. Keep going and you'll finally reach a bridge that goes over Taughannock Creek, which flows into Cayuga Lake, one of the five Finger Lakes. Do you see a figure in the sheer rock face? From here, you'll also be up close and personal with one of the most scenic waterfalls in the northern mid-Atlantic region. Power up, and head back the way you came.

SCAVENGER HUNT

American chestnut

Look for the American chestnut tree's fan of toothy leaves, and, in fall, find its shiny chestnuts on the ground. This is a rare tree in the wild— "technically extinct" according to the American Chestnut Foundation—because of a killing fungus. Today they rarely grow beyond a bush or sapling. If you see one here, high five its scaly bark.

< *Castanea dentata* (from Latin *dens*, which means "toothy")

Rock layers

This rock outcrop is layers of shale and sandstone. It's made from clay and silt that settled on top of mud and hardened. Look at the stripes in the wall—can you see lines where the color changes? The upper part is shale, and the lower portion is sandstone. When water erodes this rock, the sandstone goes first, leaving a ledge above it.

< How many layers can you see?

Serviceberry

It's hard not to think of the holidays when serviceberries produce their bright, round berry-like (and edible) pomes in summer. If you find one on the ground, turn it upside down—it looks like something exploded through one end. In spring, before the berries, come pretty white flowers. Serviceberry is also known as shadbush.

Red berries follow serviceberry blooms >

Mini falls and rainbow trout

In spring, rainbow trout make their way upstream to these falls. The rocks that form these falls, part of a 14-foot layer of limestone, are constantly eroding—but not very quickly. Because the water here is not acidic, limestone erosion occurs at a slow pace.

< Look for *Oncorhynchus mykiss* in the water

ADVENTURES IN
PENNSYLVANIA

Adventurers,

let's explore "Penn's Woods" (*sylvania* means "forest land" in Latin), which became a state in 1787 and is today nearly 60 percent forest. We'll begin by surveying the land from a tower, checking out some old iron mines, and climbing a mountain near the Appalachian Trail. We'll then continue onward, walking over suspension bridges and crossing through a dark tunnel that trains once traveled, before sliding along some rocks in water to cool off. We'll visit an old furnace, take a shower in special mineral springs, and walk out on a bridge to nowhere. We'll continue through to Pennsylvania's Grand Canyon for some views, check out eighteen waterfalls on one trail, and even make some rocks sing with a hammer. We'll be on State Park, County Park, and even National Park land. Pennsylvania's state slogan is "Pursue Your Happiness"— let's find ours in these woods!

20

SURVEY THE LAND FROM GOV. DICK OBSERVATION TOWER

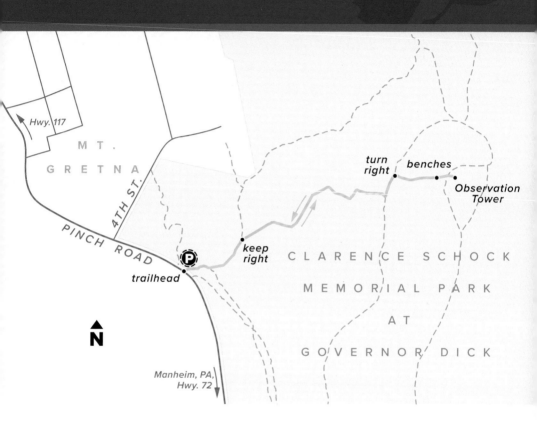

Hwy. 117

M T .
G R E T N A

4TH ST.

PINCH ROAD

P

trailhead

keep
right

turn
right

benches

Observation
Tower

C L A R E N C E   S C H O C K

M E M O R I A L   P A R K

A T

G O V E R N O R   D I C K

N

Manheim, PA,
Hwy. 72

YOUR ADVENTURE

Adventurers, our goal is to take in the view of our kingdom atop the 66-foot-tall concrete observation tower built in 1954 on the historical homeland of the Lenape. Start in the parking lot north of the Environmental Center, where you'll find two yellow gates, a bench, and a restroom. From there, go around the yellow gate on the left—this is the shortest route to the

∧ **Your goal atop Governor Dick Hill**

LENGTH

1 mile out and back

HIKE + EXPLORE 1 hour

DIFFICULTY Moderate—short, but follows a steeper, rockier route. Check for ticks after the hike.

SEASON Year-round. Each season has its beauty: wildflowers in spring, summer shade, autumn colors, and no-sweat hiking in winter.

GET THERE From I-76, take exit 266 to PA-72 / Lebanon Road and turn right. Turn right on Cider Press Road for half a mile then right onto Pinch Road for 2 miles. The parking lot will be on your right.

Google Maps: bit.ly/governordick

RESTROOM At parking lot

FEE None

TREAT YOURSELF After the climb up, head to the century-old Jigger Shop in Mount Gretna for a frozen hot chocolate or a campfire s'more sundae (served flaming!).

Clarence Schock Memorial Park at Governor Dick, Lebanon County Parks and Recreation (717) 964-3808
Facebook @LebanonParksandRec

Observation Tower. You'll follow the red blazes to the slightly steep and rocky shot right up the hill. Walk a short bit on the level ground, then turn right for your final push up to the Observation Tower and meadow. Once there, power up on one of the many benches (can you count them all?). Carefully enter the tower and follow the "Up" side, slowly climbing up each short ladder. Take in the views of all of Lebanon and Lancaster Counties and pretend this is all your kingdom! What would you do if you were a king or queen for a day? Return the way you came—straight down—watching your footing on the slippery rocks.

SCAVENGER HUNT

Witch hazel

Look for this spiky flower in fall. Its petals are small little strips. Take some construction paper at home, cut it into small strips, and try to make a witch hazel flower for your hiking partner!

< *Hamamelis virginiana*

Nine ladders inside the Observation Tower

How many ladders does it take to get to the top? Try to count how many rungs you climb in total. From the top you can see five different counties, along with Blue Mountain to the north and Mount Joy to the south. If the trees are bare, you can see features of Hershey Park and Roundtop Mountain Resort.

One step at a time! >

Mushrooms

How many of these scaly fungi can you find on the side of a tree? They can grow in the cracks or wounds of a tree.

< Look carefully on the trees and you might find this mushroom

Spicebush

Flowering spicebush in spring makes the park glow yellow. It smells good too! Take a whiff and describe the aroma to your hiking partner. Look for its red berries in summer.

Lindera benzoin >

Pileated woodpecker

This redhead is hard to miss! Listen for the *tunk-tunk-tunk* in the distance as it pecks at dead trees and trunks looking for a gourmet ant meal. You can even spot the holes it leaves behind—these become homes for many other species. What is something you do that helps other people?

Dryocopus pileatus >

21

SEARCH FOR BATS AT P. JOSEPH RAAB PARK

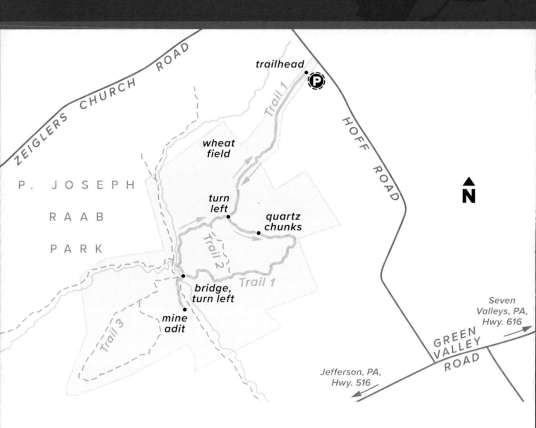

YOUR ADVENTURE

Adventurers, today we're walking exactly where the York Iron Company Mine operated from 1854–1888. You'll start off on a nice, flat, grassy trail with a bounty of wheat blowing in the wind. You'll then dip down into the forest until you reach a fork with Trail 1 to the left and Trail 2 to the right. We'll go to the left. Peek at your feet while you're on the Quartz Highway,

LENGTH

2.4-mile

lollipop loop

800–

ELEV [FT]

400–

Elevation Gain

85ft.

1   2   3   4

DISTANCE [MI]

HIKE + EXPLORE 1.5 hours

DIFFICULTY Moderate—short, but with a little bit of elevation gain and a slightly rocky pathway

SEASON Year-round

GET THERE Heading south on PA-616, turn right on Zeiglers Church Road. After 2.4 miles, turn left on Hoff Road to find the small parking lot on your right.

Google Maps: bit.ly/pjosephraab

RESTROOMS None

FEE None

TREAT YOURSELF Grab a pint of old-fashioned ice cream at Carman's just 15 minutes east in Loganville.

P. Joseph Raab Park,
York County Parks
(717) 840-7440
Facebook @YorkCountyParks

Can you see the bats from beyond the bat cage?

then find yourself at the intersection with Trail 2. Take a left here to stay on Trail 1. You'll come to a T-shaped intersection where you will head left on Trail 1 to explore the mine. Feel free to take your first left up a small hill to look in the pipe; do you see anything? Come back down, continue left, and stop at the bridge and un-named creek, where you'll have arrived at a large mine. What would you name this creek? Why? Feel the cold whoosh up against your face as you peer in to look for one of four bat species. After powering up at the creek, return the way you came, but instead of turning right stay straight to hike through a beautiful flower meadow. From there you'll run into the first trail intersection from the beginning of your hike; head left and back to the parking lot.

SCAVENGER HUNT

Ebony jewelwing damselfly
Look for this insect's black wings and metallic green body. Watch closely—it will actually turn its head to look at you! Play damselfly tag with your hiking partners and try to mimic the insects' flight pattern.

< *Calopteryx maculata*

Mine adit
There are five mine openings at the park: four horizontal, called adits, and one vertical. Today we'll explore two. The shafts were built with dynamite and hand tools. Have you ever used tools to build something?

< An adit is a horizontal mine opening

Quartz

Pretend you can hear the sound of picks, shovels, hammers, and chisels from miners as they remove 10–20 tons of ore every day. The miners were paid $0.25/week for their 8–10 hours of daily work.

You might find these quartz pieces poking out of the ground >

Little brown bat

You might get lucky and see one of the few little brown bats that are left out of the four bat species that reside in the park. The "bat doors" in front of the mines allow bats in and out. Sadly, many bats in the park have succumbed to a disease called white-nose syndrome.

Myotis lucifugus >

Mock strawberry

Look for this plant's yellow flowers and fuzzy leaves of three—"real" strawberries have white flowers. It fruits in early summer; look closely to spot the five bracts (small leaves just below the fruit). Mock strawberry's seeds stick *way* out; see if you can count them!

< *Potentilla indica*

22

SUMMIT POLE STEEPLE LIKE AN APPALACHIAN THRU-HIKER

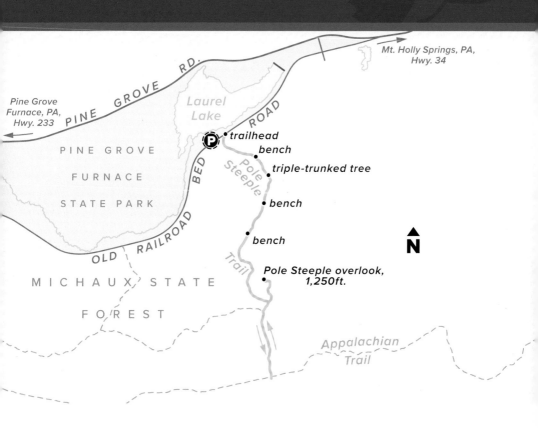

Pine Grove Furnace, PA, Hwy. 233

PINE GROVE RD.

Mt. Holly Springs, PA, Hwy. 34

Laurel Lake

ROAD

P trailhead

PINE GROVE

bench

BED

triple-trunked tree

Pole Steeple

FURNACE

bench

STATE PARK

bench

N

OLD RAILROAD

Trail

Pole Steeple overlook, 1,250ft.

MICHAUX STATE

FOREST

Appalachian Trail

YOUR ADVENTURE

Adventurers, you're about to sample the Appalachian Trail (or AT), one of the longest hiking trails in the world! This area is considered the half-way point. From the parking lot, cross the road, get some quick stretching in, and begin the short but relentless climb on the historical homeland of the Susquehannock. While hiking, keep an eye out for the blue blazes painted

LENGTH

1.9 miles

out and back

ELEV [FT]

1,300–

800

1   2   3   4

DISTANCE [MI]

Elevation Gain

539ft.

HIKE + EXPLORE 1.5 hours

DIFFICULTY Challenging—short hike but elevation gain is almost constant on the way up. Plenty of wooden benches for power-up stops.

SEASON Year-round

GET THERE From I-81, take PA-34 south about 8 miles, then a slight right on Green Mountain Road. Continue onto Pine Grove Road for 4 miles, then make a slight left onto Old Railroad Bed Road. In half a mile, the parking lot will be on the right and the trail across the street.

Google Maps: bit.ly/polesteeple

RESTROOMS None at trailhead, but the lodge has some just down the road

FEE None

TREAT YOURSELF Make like a thru-hiker and try the Half-Gallon Challenge at the Pine Grove General Store, just 7 minutes east on Bendersville Road. Or get yourself a reasonable cone and watch the hikers give it a shot instead.

Pine Grove Furnace State Park, Pennsylvania Department of Conservation and Natural Resources
(717) 486-7174
Facebook @PADCNR

Carefully step on the pulpit!

on the trees—if you don't see them, you may have lost the trail. Also keep an eye out for a triple-trunked tree as you continue onward. Take a power-up on the two log benches and get ready for the long climb up the rock stairs. Can you count them all? You'll eventually reach a "T" in the road. Go to the left for 0.2 miles to reach Pole Steeple. Power up here by taking a seat on the quartzite outcropping on the top of Piney Mountain (be careful and stay back from the edge); watch for birds of prey easily soaring above you. When your energy returns, go back down the hill and continue following the double-blazed trees that extend all the way to a junction with the AT. Touch the white blaze, look both ways, and try to spot a thru-hiker. Head back down the way you came. Consider staying the night at one of the campgrounds in the state park and be sure to take a dip in Laurel Lake in summer.

SCAVENGER HUNT

Turkey vulture
Look for the silhouette of the turkey vulture—you should see a narrow tail and long, straight wings with what look like fingers on the ends. Watch its flying pattern—what does it look like it's doing?

< *Cathartes aura*

Appalachian Trail white blaze
Touch the blaze and look both ways. Do you see any thru-hikers (people who hike the full trail)? Think of how many miles you hiked today—could you complete a long-distance hike? Describe how that might feel to your hiking partner.

The famous white blaze of the 2,190-mile-long AT >

Mountain laurel

Look for the shiny leaves of this evergreen shrub year-round and its white cup-like flowers in spring. Get a close look at the shape of the flowers and their red spots, then take a piece of paper from your nature journal and try to fold and color the paper to look like the laurel's flower!

Kalmia latifolia, Pennsylvania's state flower >

Pitch pine cone

Why do some of the pine cones you find seem closed and smooth like this one, and others open? When it's warm, the cone automatically opens, like a lock, to release its seeds. It stays snapped shut when it's cold. Why do you think that is? Use your fingers or a rock to try to pry one open and see what you find inside.

< Cone of *Pinus rigida*

Quartzite summit

The northeast-dipping rocks around you are more than 550 million years old! Look for the vertical slabs that are evidence of a fault zone where the rock experienced a lot of pressure and split, the two sides moving opposite each other. What else do you notice about the summit?

This gray quartzite is a kind of metamorphic (transformed by heat or pressure) rock >

23

CROSS THE BRIDGE TO BALANCED ROCK AT TROUGH CREEK

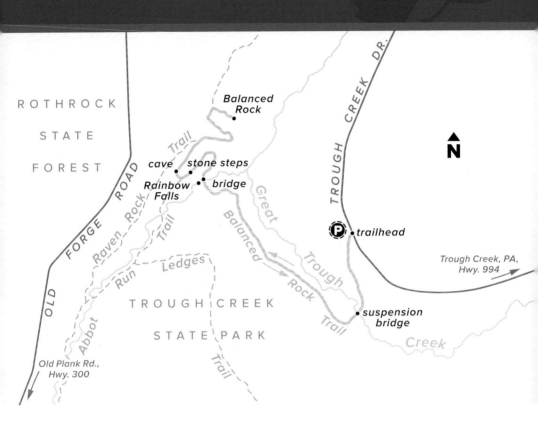

ROTHROCK

STATE

FOREST

Balanced Rock

Trail

cave   stone steps

Rainbow   • bridge
Falls

ROAD

FORGE

Raven Rock

Trail

OLD

Run

Ledges

Abbot

Trail

TROUGH CREEK

STATE PARK

Balanced

Rock

Great

Trough

Trough

TROUGH CREEK DR.

N

P   • trailhead

Trough Creek, PA,
Hwy. 994

• suspension
bridge

Creek

Old Plank Rd.,
Hwy. 300

YOUR ADVENTURE

Great Trough Creek runs for 33.2 miles through the historical homeland of the Susquehannock, and we'll kick things off on the suspension bridge that hovers over it. After a short walk, take a rest at the bench by Rainbow Falls and cross another bridge (can you tell the difference between this bridge and the suspension bridge?). Head up the stone steps built by the Civilian

LENGTH

1 mile

out and back

ELEV [FT]

1,100–

700–

Elevation
Gain
90ft.

DISTANCE [MI]

1   2   3   4

HIKE + EXPLORE 1 hour

DIFFICULTY Easy—short hike full of surprises; some stairs, but they are short

SEASON Year-round. Spring, or after a rain, is best for waterfall flow; summer brings great rhododendron blooms; winter is beautiful and quiet; and fall is all brilliant colors.

GET THERE From PA-26 / Raystown Road head east on PA-994 / New Plank Road for 5 miles. Turn left on Logging Road 31118 for 2 miles then left onto Trough Creek Drive. After 2 miles, the parking lot will be on your left.

Google Maps: bit.ly/timbertrough

RESTROOMS None at trailhead, but there is one at the main parking lot

FEE None

TREAT YOURSELF Mamie's Cafe in Martinsburg has pastries, donuts, hot cocoa, and yummy breakfast and lunch.

Trough Creek State Park,
Pennsylvania Department of Conservation
and Natural Resources
(814) 658-3847
Facebook @PADCNR

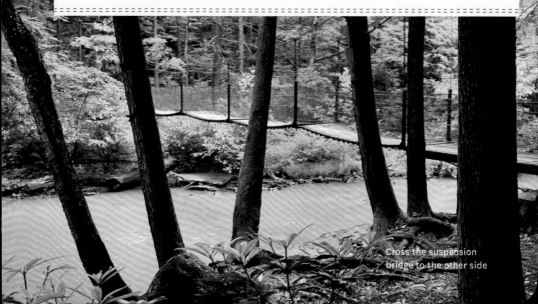

Cross the suspension
bridge to the other side

Conservation Corps to check out a sweet cave (careful on the scramble). Keep going to see Middle and Upper Rainbow Falls—power up here and take a look at your surroundings. From here you can turn right at the top of the steps to continue up to Balanced Rock. Examine the rock from all sides before heading back the way you came. Make a stop at the Ice Mine on your way out of the park.

SCAVENGER HUNT

Hydrangea

Hydrangeas, like many other plants, *love* water; how much water do you drink every day? Can you count how many individual petals this fragrant flower has?

Hydor means "water" and *angeion* means "vessel"—the seed pods look like water jugs! >

Rainbow Falls

Rainbow Falls looks like a series of stairs that run downward to Great Trough Creek. It originates at Abbott Run and is best seen after a rain or in spring.

12-foot staircase falls >

Cave

Seek refuge in this cave on your way up the trail. What kind of erosion could have caused this? Look closely as you crawl inside. Where does the water go?

< The result of erosion

Great rhododendron

Look for this evergreen shrub and its leathery leaves as you explore the area. Its white and purple flowers come out in June and July in clusters of five petals.

< *Rhododendron maximum*

Balanced Rock

Trough Creek cut this valley millions of years ago and this sandstone block has not moved from its original position. It broke away from rock cliffs and other rocks around it eroded away, leaving it on this cliff edge.

< How long do you think Balanced Rock will stay perched here? It's what's known as an erosion remnant.

24

BRAVE THE TUNNEL ON THE ALLEGHENY PORTAGE RAILROAD

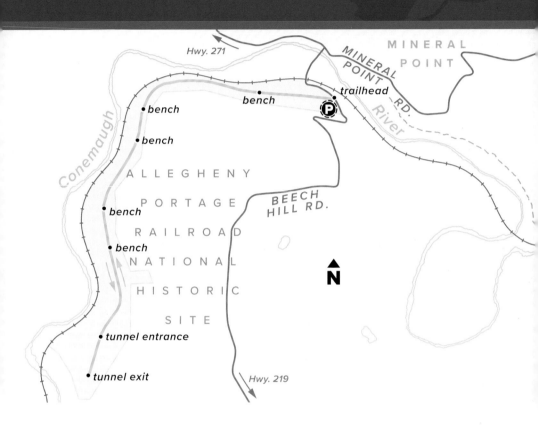

Hwy. 271

MINERAL POINT

MINERAL POINT

trailhead

MINERAL POINT RD.

River

bench

bench

bench

Conemaugh

A L L E G H E N Y

P O R T A G E

BEECH HILL RD.

bench

R A I L R O A D

bench

N A T I O N A L

H I S T O R I C

S I T E

N

tunnel entrance

tunnel exit

Hwy. 219

YOUR ADVENTURE

Adventurers, ready to take the Tunnel Challenge? Your destination today is America's first railroad tunnel, the Staple Bend Tunnel, finished in 1834. The 70-mile trail starts off nice and flat under a canopy of oaks and maples on the Conemaugh River. Stop and power up at each bench—can you count them all?—and explore the rippling water coming from the streams on your

LENGTH

4.4 miles

out and back

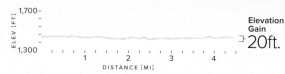

Elevation
Gain
20ft.

HIKE + EXPLORE 2 hours

DIFFICULTY Challenging—old rail trail with easy terrain (suitable for strollers) but it can be long for littles. There are many benches and interesting things to see on the way, so take your time and power up as needed.

SEASON Year-round.

GET THERE From Highway 22, take the PA-271 exit and head south for 5 miles. Turn left on Mineral Point Road then right on Beech Hill Road. The park entrance will be on your right.

Google Maps: bit.ly/staplebend

RESTROOMS At parking lot

FEE None

TREAT YOURSELF Fox's Pizza Den is just 10 minutes away—be sure to try their heart-shaped pepperonis.

Allegheny Portage Railroad National Historic Site, National Park Service
(814) 886-6150
Facebook @alleghenyportagerrnps

Are you brave enough to walk through to the other side?

left. Look closely: the water travels through pipes and out the other side to prevent flooding of the tracks. Every time you pass a half-mile marker, stop and give your hiking partner a high-five! After the 1-mile marker, there is an optional small, short trail that leads to a culvert. Finally, at a little over 2 miles, you'll find the Staple Bend Tunnel. Peer into it—you should be able to see a faint light on the other end. Grab your hiking partner's hand and, if you dare, try to make it to the other side (about 0.2 miles). If you want, you can use your cellphone flashlight to light the way. Compare the two entrances and head back the way you came.

SCAVENGER HUNT

Front of tunnel

Miners chipped and blasted through 901 feet of rock to make this tunnel. It cost $37,498.85—how long would it take you to earn that much with your allowance? They started digging in 1831 and finished nineteen months later, chipping away only 18 inches of rock each day.

< How does the entrance differ from the inside?

Sleeper stones

Sleeper stones, a concept borrowed from England, were used as a foundation for the rails on level sections. They were dug into the ground, flush with the surface. Each stone took 24 hours to cut and shape and almost 200,000 of them were created for the project!

The rails sat on the chairs with iron wedges and wooden plugs >

Purple-flowering raspberry

Look for the rounded purple petals of this shrub in summer. Take some scissors and paper at home and try to cut out a replica of the flower. Watch for its five-lobed leaves to turn yellow in fall.

< *Rubus odoratus*

Culverts

In total, there were 68 culverts on the Allegheny Portage Railroad that were built in the early 1830s. Two historic culverts are located on the Staple Bend Tunnel Trail. The culverts were used for drainage and allowed water to pass underneath the railroad bed, which allowed the timber foundations to last through years of being wet.

One of two culverts you can see on this hike >

25

ROCK-HOP ALONG MEADOW RUN TO OHIOPYLE SLIDES

YOUR ADVENTURE

Adventurers, today we journey on the historical homeland of the Monongahela. You'll begin by heading down a staircase that takes you to Meadow Run, a tributary of the 134-mile Youghiogheny River. Starting right in at Ohiopyle Slides, follow the orange blazes, taking it all in before you continue to rock hop along the run. You'll dip back into the woods and then

LENGTH

2.8 miles out and back

ELEV [FT]

1,500 –

1,100 –

Elevation
Gain
196ft.

1   2   3   4

DISTANCE [MI]

HIKE + EXPLORE 2 hours

DIFFICULTY Challenging—after a rain the rocky path can turn muddy and slippery, and the trail can at times be hard to follow

SEASON Year-round. Popular in summer for the natural rock waterslides. Avoid after a big rain; can be slippery in winter.

GET THERE Take Main Street / PA-381 northeast from Farmington. The parking lot will be on your right at the intersection with Ohiopyle Road.

Google Maps: bit.ly/timberohiopyle

RESTROOMS At parking lot

FEE None

TREAT YOURSELF Grab some ice cream at the Ohiopyle Old Mill General Store just down the street.

Ohiopyle State Park, Pennsylvania Department of Conservation and Natural Resources
(724) 329-8591
Facebook @OhiopyleSP

∧ Rush like the water over the rocks

wind back again along the river rocks. Cross a sweet bridge and make your way to a big flat rock. Power up here and keep on trucking until you reach Cascades Waterfall. Power up here and head back the way you came. Be sure to check out nearby Cucumber Falls and the Ohiopyle State Park Visitor Center. There is camping nearby if you want to make a weekend of it.

SCAVENGER HUNT

Rhododendron tunnels

As the trail meanders away from Meadow Run, you'll come across the rhododendron tunnels! Walk through them and take a big whiff. Feel their leathery leaves and look for their clusters of flowers, often the first to bloom in spring.

< Rhododendron maximum

Cascades Waterfall

Meadow Run is a 14-mile tributary of the Youghiogheny River, which is a 134-mile tributary of the Monongahela River, which is 130 miles long and feeds into the 981-mile-long Ohio River. One leaf dropped here could make it all the way to Kentucky!

< Watch the rambling water

Ebony spleenwort fern

Run your hands over this fern's fingerlike pinnae (leaflets). How many can you count? The plant's name is a reference to its use in treating spleen issues. Do you know where your spleen is located?

< *Asplenium platyneuron*

Flat rock

Take a power-up break—carefully—on this flat rock that is over 300 million years old! It has been eroded by the water around it to take this shape. Rub the rock and imagine the kind of force needed to sand this down.

Flat, smooth homewood sandstone >

Yellow patches mushroom

Look closely underneath the mushroom—how many gills can you count? The stalk is called a stipe. How tall do you think the stipe is on this one?

< *Amanita flavoconia*

26

RUN UP ROCK FURNACE TO THE SUSPENSION BRIDGE

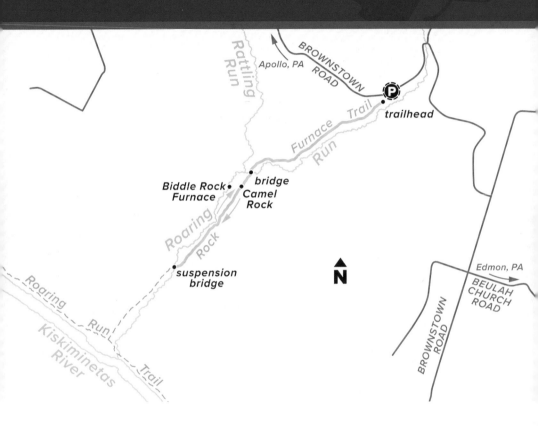

YOUR ADVENTURE

Adventurers, today we're on the historical homeland of the Massawom-ack and heading toward the Kiskiminetas River, a 27-mile tributary of the Allegheny River. Historically, the Kiskiminetas River has been one of the most polluted river systems in the state. In recent years however, it has seen a tremendous recovery thanks to the efforts of many environmental

LENGTH

2 miles

out and back

ELEV [FT] 1,100–

700

Elevation Gain
194ft.

DISTANCE [MI]   1   2   3   4

HIKE + EXPLORE 1.5 hours

DIFFICULTY Moderate—trail is flat, but there is some gentle elevation gain on the way back

SEASON Year-round

GET THERE Take Old State Road east from Apollo and turn right onto Jackson Road for 1 mile. Continue onto Brownstown Road, and in less than a mile (before the intersection with McCartney Road) find the parking lot on your right.

Google Maps: bit.ly/rockfurnace

RESTROOMS None

FEE None

TREAT YOURSELF Sweetlane Chocolate in Vandergrift has fun chocolates, hand-made milkshakes, and seasonal treats.

Roaring Run Watershed Association, Trans Allegheny Trails
(724) 681-6317
Instagram @RoaringRunWatershed

Clamber across the bridge

partners within the Kiski-Conemaugh River Basin. Start out on the flat, wide trail and you'll soon come upon Rattling Run. Cross a small railroad tie bridge and continue to follow Roaring Run, powering up at a bench on your right. Pass by the site of the former Biddle Rock Furnace, one of the first iron furnaces in Pennsylvania, in operation from 1825–1850. Keep going until you reach the suspension bridge. Cross over Roaring Run, power up, and head back to where you started.

SCAVENGER HUNT

Pickerel frog

Look for the brown spots on the back of this amphibian who likes to hang out along Roaring Run. This frog is carnivorous and loves snacking on bugs and other invertebrates. Don't touch it! It protects itself by shedding a poisonous chemical. If you visit during spring you might find an egg cluster with up to 3,000 eggs.

< *Lithobates palustris*

Biddle Rock Furnace

Can you see this furnace's stone walls? It was once fueled by charcoal from this very forest (they cut down about an acre each day!), and limestone and iron ore were mined from the surrounding hills.

< This museum model shows what the furnace once looked like

Jack-in-the-pulpit

Look along the trail for this unique hooded flower blooming from April to June. A cluster of red berries will follow in summer. Pull your hood over your head and try to make yourself look like Jack!

< *Arisaema triphyllum*

Camel Rock

Look closely at the flakes of this sandstone—can you see birch seedlings growing out of it? What will happen to the rock if these continue to grow? Sketch it in your journal. Do you think the rock looks like a camel?

Sandstone boulder >

Cable suspension bridge

Sketch this suspension bridge in your nature journal. How do you think they built this all the way out here? How long would it take?

72 feet long >

27

FEEL THE WATER AT MINERAL SPRINGS

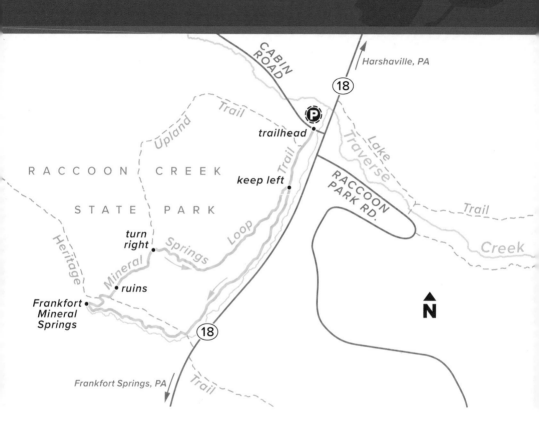

CABIN ROAD

Harshaville, PA

18

trailhead

Upland Trail

RACCOON CREEK

keep left

Loop Trail

STATE PARK

Lake Traverse

RACCOON PARK RD.

Trail

Creek

turn right

Springs

Heritage

Mineral

ruins

Frankfort Mineral Springs

18

N

Frankfort Springs, PA

Trail

YOUR ADVENTURE

Adventurers, today we're on the historical homeland of the Shawnee and Lenape. In the 1930s, President Franklin D. Roosevelt formed the Civilian Conservation Corps to establish recreation centers near big cities like Pittsburgh and this led to the creation of Raccoon Creek State Park. From the gravel parking area, you'll see a post indicating a trail on the lefthand side—follow it straight ahead. Keep straight and pass the Heritage Trail;

LENGTH

1.2-mile

lollipop loop

Elevation Gain
209ft.

HIKE + EXPLORE 1.5 hours

DIFFICULTY Moderate—lovely meandering loop with very little elevation gain, but there are some roots and rocks to watch out for along the way. After a rain it can be muddy and possibly flooded, so call ahead in wet weather.

SEASON Year-round. Winter is particularly beautiful.

GET THERE Take PA-18 north from Frankfort Springs for about 2 miles and turn left on Cabin Road to find the parking area.

Google Maps: bit.ly/timbermineral

RESTROOMS None

FEE None

TREAT YOURSELF Janoski's Farm and Greenhouse, 7 miles east on Lincoln Highway, serves fresh fruit, baked goods, and more.

Raccoon Creek State Park,
Pennsylvania Department of Conservation and Natural Resources
(724) 899-2200
Facebook @RaccoonCreekStatePark

This was the site of a resort and spa in the 1800s

turn right on Mineral Springs Loop Trail when you reach the creek. Hike that way for a bit; you'll cross a wooden bridge over the creek and eventually reach another bridge and the grotto. Power up here and take in the view of Frankfort Mineral Springs Waterfall and the springs on the right. Set off again and continue past the falls to visit the ruins of the former visitor center (demolished after it was vandalized). Turn right to continue on Mineral Springs Loop Trail (passing the Upland Trail). Soon you'll make it back to that first fork you passed when you began, where you can turn left and return to the parking lot. Camping is available at Raccoon Creek State Park if you want to make a night of it.

SCAVENGER HUNT

Resort ruins

Edward McGinnis built and ran a resort and health spa here throughout much of the 1800s and early 1900s. A fire eventually forced the place to close and the remains have mostly been reclaimed by nature. Draw in your nature journal what it once might have looked like.

< Can you imagine a resort here?

Seasonal special: great white trillium

Look for these magical flowers in spring. They can live up to twenty-five years! Can you count the three petals and the three green sepals just below the flower? They love living in the woods because of the shade. Do you prefer sunlight or shade?

Trillium grandiflorum >

Frankfort Mineral Springs Falls

This bowl that you're standing in is a grotto. See if you can stand behind the falls. The creeks from the grotto all run to feed nearby Raccoon Lake. Run your hands through the water— do you feel its magical properties?

< 8- to 10-foot falls made up of shale and sandstone

Mineral Springs

This spring water comes from an underground reservoir. Visitors to the resort in the 1800s believed that the water could help cure things like tummy aches. The water now has a strange orange tint as a result of the high iron content (you can see evidence of this on the cave's rocks), so please don't drink from it unless you have a water filter.

The mineral iron tints the rocks orange >

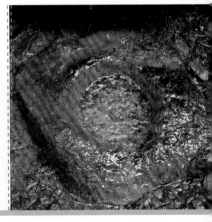

28

OBSERVE FROM THE DECK ON THE TAMARACK TRAIL

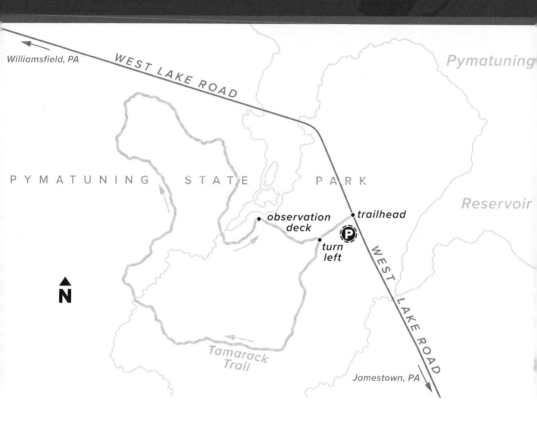

YOUR ADVENTURE

Adventurers, today we're on the historical homeland of the Haudenosaunee and Lenape. The name Pymatuning means "crooked-mouth man's dwelling place"; where do you think the name came from? Dams like this one get built for many reasons—hydroelectricity, recreation, or, in this case, flood prevention. Imagine being one of the 7,000 workers who created this dam and reservoir over the course of three years. The trailhead is easy to miss,

LENGTH

1.3-mile

lollipop loop

ELEV [FT]

1,300 –

900

Elevation
Gain

22ft.

DISTANCE [MI]

1   2   3   4

HIKE + EXPLORE 1 hour

DIFFICULTY Easy—red blazes mark your loop the entire way with little elevation gain. After a rain, bridges can be slippery and the muddy trail can slow you down.

SEASON Year-round. Tamarack trees are beautiful in fall.

GET THERE From Highway 322, take West Lake Road for about a mile. Trailhead parking is on the west side of the road (the opposite side from the lake), just south of the Century Club.

Google Maps: bit.ly/timberpymatuning

RESTROOMS None

FEE None

TREAT YOURSELF Just down the road, Jamestown Hunger Buster has twenty-four flavors of Perry's hard scoop. 'Nuff said.

Pymatuning State Park,
Pennsylvania Department of Conservation and Natural Resources
(724) 932-3141
Facebook @PymatuningStatePark

What can you see from the observation deck?

so keep your eyes open for a small grassy parking lot and a trail sign after you drive past the Century Club. Start out on the Tamarack Trail, and when you get to a junction, head left to walk the loop clockwise. Listen carefully as you walk—there is so much life in the canopy above you! Power up at a bench right away, cross a couple of bridges, and wind your way through this hardwood forest, which is often full of mushrooms. Take the short spur trail and power up on the viewing platform. Turn left at the next intersection to return to the trailhead.

SCAVENGER HUNT

Seasonal special: multiflora rose

From May to June, look for these clusters of yummy-smelling white flowers. They have five petals and bright yellow pollen. Red fruits called hips will replace the flowers in summer. Multiflora rose is non-native and invasive in the region, but charming nonetheless.

Rosa multiflora >

Skunk cabbage

Look for these huge green leaves by the boardwalk. Take a whiff—skunk cabbage emits a yucky smell (like rotting meat!) to attract certain bugs that like that kind of thing. The flowers stick high up with a hood called a spathe and have a knob inside called a spadix. Look closely–it has a bunch of petal-less flowers.

< *Symplocarpus foetidus* (*foetidus* means "stinky" in Latin)

Snail

Look carefully for sticky slime trails, which help snails move over difficult terrain like this bumpy tree bark. Do your best snail interpretation for your hiking buddy.

< Keep an eye out for this gastropod

Deer tracks

Keep a close eye on the ground—it holds many secrets about wildlife! Deer tracks will resemble upside-down hearts (an impression of their two toes). How far apart are the tracks? Which direction were they heading? Were they running?

< Can you spot the hooves?

29

FOLLOW THE OLD SIDEWALK AT PRESQUE ISLE STATE PARK

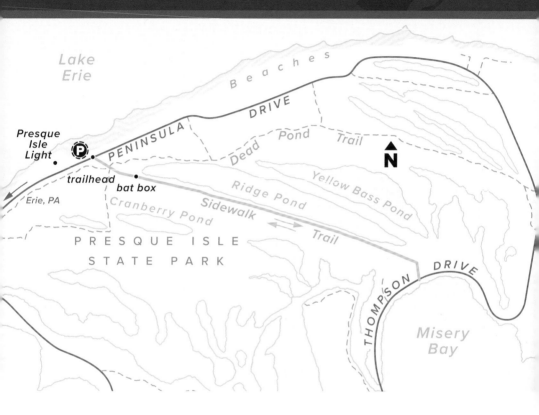

YOUR ADVENTURE

Adventurers, get ready to hike this sandy peninsula (land covered on three sides by water—*almost* an island, which is what *presque isle* means in French) on some of Pennsylvania's only shoreline. On this historical homeland of the Erie, you can find up to 48 species of mammals, 108 species of native fish, and over 320 species of birds! You're going to head out today on the historic Sidewalk Trail, which stretches all the way out to Misery Bay.

LENGTH

2.5 miles

out and back

HIKE + EXPLORE 1.5 hours

DIFFICULTY Easy—old concrete sidewalk

SEASON Year-round. Trail can be overgrown after rains, so always check for ticks after your hike. Water level can sometimes be high, so check in with park staff at the Tom Ridge Environmental Center before you begin your hike.

GET THERE From the entrance sign to the park, follow signs for Presque Isle Lighthouse until you reach the parking lot and the signs for Leslie Beach.

Google Maps: bit.ly/timbersidewalk

RESTROOM At parking lot

FEE None; $7 if you want to tour the lighthouse and climb the tower (would recommend!)

TREAT YOURSELF Grab some cookies at Art's Bakery in Erie. Sara's Restaurant (open in summer), near the park's entrance, is another good option.

Presque Isle State Park
(814) 833-7424 | Facebook @PresqueIslePA

The rare Pennsylvania "coast"!

The US Lighthouse Service created this path to connect the light station to a boathouse on Misery Bay. It was much safer to cart supplies along the walkway than have a ship or boat attempt to unload on the beach in front of the Light Station. This used to be a wooden boardwalk but was resurfaced with concrete in 1925. Notice the different ecological zones along the trail, from forest to wetland to scrub and underbrush. You'll soon pass a bat box, which houses bats in spring and summer. The trail eventually bends to the right for the last leg, which will take you to the road at Misery Bay. Once you reach Thompson Drive and Misery Bay, power up with some lunch and head back the way you came. Be sure to check out the lighthouse and the nearby Tom Ridge Environmental Center before you leave.

SCAVENGER HUNT

Sidewalk

While you trek along the sidewalk, imagine you are carrying supplies from Misery Bay to the lighthouse. How would you carry them? What kind of supplies would you be carrying?

< This was once a raised plank trail before the sidewalk was installed in 1925

Light station

This still-functioning light station (not technically a lighthouse because there are other buildings attached) is maintained by the US Coast Guard. The brick tower is 57 feet tall. Do you think you could manage a lighthouse? What kind of skills and knowledge do you think that would take? Consider climbing to the top of the tower at the end of your hike.

< Built in 1872 and lit in 1873

Spring peeper

The chirping call of the spring peeper is a hallmark of the season, but few will see the tiny (about 1.25 inches long) frog as it clings to the side of a tree to emit that distinctive sound. Its tan to dark brown color changes to better match surrounding vegetation and daylight conditions. Draw this camouflaging frog in your nature journal.

Pseudacris crucifer >

Pickerel frog

This amphibian looks like a leopard frog—can you guess why? In the spring mating season, pickerel frogs gather at temporary pools in forests and fields, so look for them there. They are the only poisonous frogs native to the United States. Their skin secretions are toxic to some of their predators, such as larger frogs, but more of an irritation to others, including humans—still, don't pick them up if you see them.

Lithobates palustris >

Common snapping turtle

This is among the largest of all the turtle species on Presque Isle. Common snapping turtles are relatively harmless in water, but can become quite aggressive and dangerous while on land if they are disturbed, so be careful. Why do you think they snap?

Chelydra serpentina >

30

FACE THE ROCKS ON THE RIMROCK TRAIL

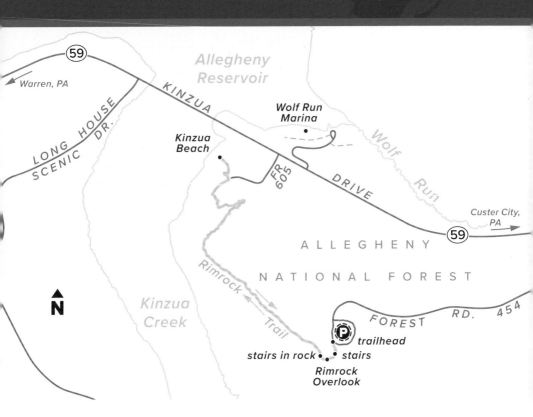

Allegheny Reservoir

59

Warren, PA

KINZUA

LONG HOUSE SCENIC DR.

Wolf Run Marina

Kinzua Beach

FR 605

Wolf Run

DRIVE

Custer City, PA

59

ALLEGHENY

NATIONAL FOREST

Kinzua Creek

Rimrock Trail

FOREST RD. 454

N

P trailhead

stairs in rock • • stairs

Rimrock Overlook

YOUR ADVENTURE

Adventurers, it's time to become ruler of a rock castle atop a hill on the historical homeland of the Seneca. Take in the views of the Allegheny Reservoir and then begin the gradual downhill hike to Kinzua Beach. Pass all the cool and unique rock formations, working your way along a staircase cut through the rock while looking closely for different kinds of moss and

LENGTH

3.3 miles out and back

Elevation Gain **600ft.**

ELEV [FT]
2,000
1,300
DISTANCE [MI]
1   2   3   4

∧ Squeeze through this passage to the bottom

HIKE + EXPLORE 2 hours

DIFFICULTY Challenging—follow the white blazes. Younger children will need to stop and power up at all of benches as the climb back up is steady (good news is it's a fun ride down!).

SEASON Year-round. Cross-country skiing in winter; summer is a vista of lush green foliage and blue waters; fall color is magical.

GET THERE From PA-59 east of Warren, turn south on Forest Road at the sign for Rimrock Picnic Area Overlook and follow to the parking area at the end of the road.

Google Maps: bit.ly/timberrimrock

RESTROOMS At parking lot

FEE None

TREAT YOURSELF TJ's Corner Store, 20 minutes east in Lewis Run, has huge cones ready for your post-hike feast.

Allegheny National Forest,
Bradford Ranger District
(814) 362-4613 | Facebook @AlleghenyNF

lichen. Follow the white blazes as you head downhill. Continue, passing by benches (potential power-ups) as the wide trail gradually makes its way down. Be bear aware—try to make noise as you hike. (If you come across one, do not run! Back away calmly and slowly while making more noise so that the bear knows where you are.) Turn around and head back up the way you came.

SCAVENGER HUNT

Mountain laurel bloom
Starting in May, take in the beauty of Pennsylvania's state flower, a sign of early summer. Feel its leathery, lance-shaped evergreen leaves at any time of year.

< *Kalmia latifolia*

Lichen
Lichens are the result of a symbiotic relationship between a fungus and algae. The fungus grows on the tree and collects moisture for the algae, and the algae creates food from the sun to feed the fungus. Look carefully—can you see the relationship at work?

< Fungus + algae = lichen

Rock faces

Check out the sandstone faces made by erosion on the rock structures in the park. How many can you find? Draw your own rock face in your nature journal.

< Can you feel the cold air from here in summer?

Orange jelly mushroom

Look for this bright orange, brainlike fungus in summer and fall. When you find it, look closely at its folds. What does it resemble to you?

Dacrymyces palmatus >

Red elderberry

This shrub hangs out by the rocks. You'll first see its white flowers in early summer; these will later give way to bright red berries. How many berries can you count?

Sambucus racemosa >

31

KINZUA BRIDGE TWO WAYS

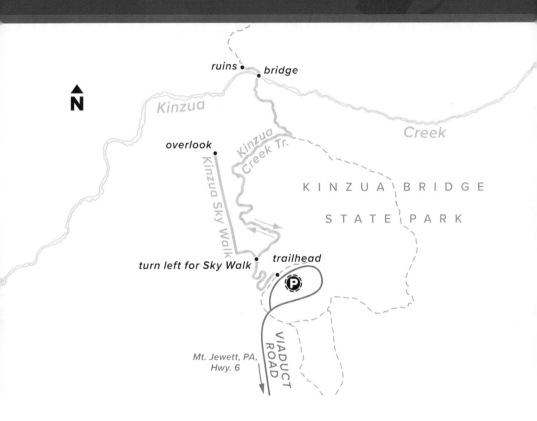

YOUR ADVENTURE

Adventurers, let's travel back in time. You'll start this hike on the historical homeland of the Seneca by bravely and carefully walking along the former viaduct (a bridge built over a valley). It was the tallest railroad bridge in the world when it was built in 1882. See if you can count the railway ties. If you can handle it, stand on the glass and peer down 225 feet below you. Close

LENGTH

1.5 miles

out and back

ELEV [FT]

2,100

1,700

Elevation Gain

292ft.

DISTANCE [MI]

1   2   3   4

HIKE + EXPLORE 1 hour

DIFFICULTY Moderate—fun downhill but killer steps on the way back up. Ground is flat and graveled and there are plenty of power-up benches (you can do it!).

SEASON Year-round. Great foliage views in fall; snowshoes available for loan in winter; the Sky Walk may be closed for frost or ice, so be sure to call before heading out.

GET THERE From Mount Jewett on Highway 6 / Main Street, turn left on Lower Lindholm Road then continue on Lindholm Road for 2.3 miles. Turn left on Viaduct Road to reach the parking lot.

Google Maps: bit.ly/timberkinzua

RESTROOMS At parking lot and visitor center

FEE None

TREAT YOURSELF Smethport Drive In is just 20 minutes away—don't miss their special Tubbers with chocolate sauce, marshmallow, and peanuts.

Kinzua Bridge State Park,
Pennsylvania Department of
Conservation and Natural Resources
(814) 778-5467
Facebook @PADCNR

< Are you ready to walk the plank?

your eyes and imagine what it must have sounded like when the tornado of 2003 took it down! Once you've left the skywalk, follow the sign for Kinzua Creek Trail. Start by descending quickly on the huge sandstone stairs, after which the trail levels out as you come across a bench and are face-to-face with the struts of the Sky Walk. Continue down into the brush until you come to the bridge over Kinzua Creek. Make a wish and look up high to where you stood just a while ago. Walk a little bit farther past the bridge to see some of the debris twisted and gnarled around you (but don't go any farther than that). When you're done looking around, head back the way you came. If you're looking for more adventure, check out the nearby Knox and Kane Rail Trails.

SCAVENGER HUNT

White-tailed deer
Go into "hush mode" for a minute—you just might spot wildlife like the white-tailed deer. Can you tell the difference between a male (buck) and female (doe)? In fall, bucks will have antlers that grow annually and eventually fall off. Look on the ground to see if you can find any.

< *Odocoileus virginianus*

Kinzua Creek Bridge
Kinzua Creek is 26.5 miles long and a tributary of the Allegheny River, which is 325 miles long. Today you're crossing a very small portion of the creek. How many steps does it take to get to the other side?

< Cross the creek

Bulbous buttercup

What's up, buttercup? This bright yellow flower is shaped like a cup. Take some paper from your nature journal and try to make your own buttercup.

< *Ranunculus bulbosus*

Broken viaduct pieces

The viaduct was partially destroyed by a tornado in 2003, which blew down the structures that held the bridge up. Look for the iron anchor bolts—these hold the bridge together but they were not up for the task during the tornado.

Behold the power of tornadoes! >

32

WALK THE RIM TO OTTER POINT

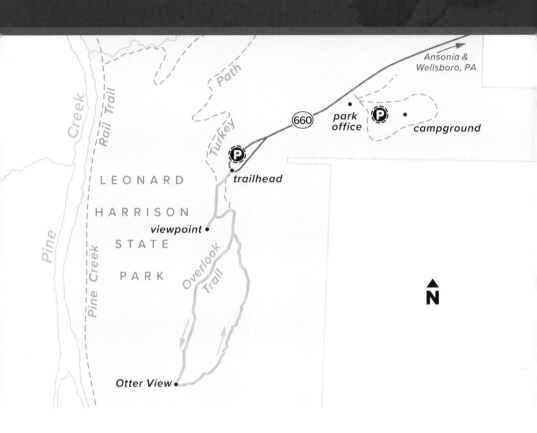

Ansonia &
Wellsboro, PA

Creek

Rail Trail

Path

Turkey

660

park
office

P

campground

P

trailhead

LEONARD

HARRISON

viewpoint •

STATE

Overlook
Trail

PARK

Pine

Pine Creek

N

Otter View •

YOUR ADVENTURE

Adventurers, let's get a good view over this 800-foot-deep gorge, known as
"Pennsylvania's Grand Canyon." It was carved by glacial meltwater 20,000
years ago, which explains why it is shaped like a big "U." The park was
named after Leonard Harrison, a businessman and banker who donated the
land to the state in 1922. Its original name was The Lookout, and it's easy

LENGTH

1-mile

lollipop loop

HIKE + EXPLORE 1 hour

DIFFICULTY Moderate—short with some rocky and rooty terrain. Small uphill slog to get back up, but several benches await your power-ups.

SEASON Closed in winter. The first three weeks of October are usually spectacular because of the high variety of deciduous trees changing color.

GET THERE From Highway 6 in Ansonia, head south on PA-362 / Pine Creek Road for 1.5 miles, turn right on the gravel road T446, then make a sharp right onto Copp Hollow Road. After 1.8 miles, turn right on Synder Point Road for 1.5 miles, then make another sharp right on PA-660 to reach the state park visitor center.

Google Maps: bit.ly/timberotter

RESTROOMS At parking lot

FEE None

TREAT YOURSELF The Yellow Basket and Ice Cream Shop is just 10 minutes east in Wellsboro—try the unicorn sundae.

Leonard Harrison State Park, Pennsylvania Department of Conservation and Natural Resources
(570) 724-3061 | Facebook @PADCNR

A short loop rewards you with this stellar view

to see why. For this hike, you'll start on the Overlook Trail, which will soon meet the canyon rim. After a quarter mile, you'll reach a sign for the lower view picnic area; head that way for a great power-up spot. Once you're fully charged, go back to Overlook Trail and follow the loop around counter-clockwise. After a stop at Otter View, continue on the loop to meet back up with where you started and return to the trailhead. On your way out you can stop at the Civilian Conservation Corps statue and pay tribute to the workers who built this park (and many others) in the 1930s.

SCAVENGER HUNT

Incinerator

In 1929, the stock market crashed and many people lost their jobs. President Franklin D. Roosevelt was elected in 1933 and soon after created the Civilian Conservation Corps (or CCC), a program that offered jobs to citizens to build great things in our country. Many of the features at this park were the result of that program.

Built in the 1930s by the Civilian Conservation Corps >

American robin

You can't miss the red chest of this worm-eater as it comes out in early spring. Listen for its beautiful whistling song and try to mimic it yourself.

< *Turdus migratorius*

Waterfall

This waterfall is unnamed—what would you call it? Write down some ideas in your nature journal and share them with your hiking partner.

< Take the short trail to this hidden waterfall

Daisy fleabane

If you come across this flower, look closely at the yellow disk in its center. Do you see what looks like a ton of little yellow mini flowers? Those are called florets, and they get pollinated to make even more flowers.

Erigeron annuus >

American beech

To find an American beech, look for these big, leathery, tooth-edged leaves on a tree with smooth bark (it stays smooth even when it's old!). Trace the toothy edges in your nature journal.

Fagus grandifolia >

33

DOUBLE THE FUN ON THE DOUBLE RUN

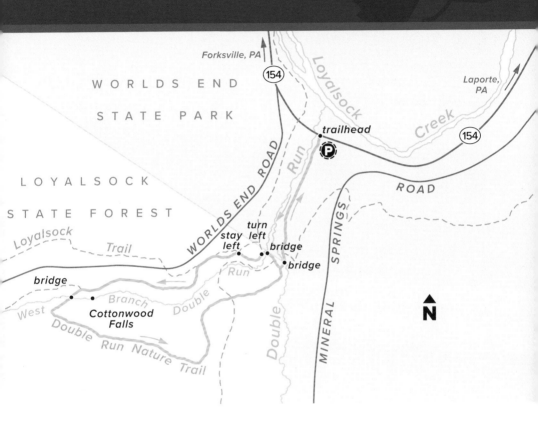

Forksville, PA

(154)

Loyalsock

WORLDS END

STATE PARK

Laporte, PA

trailhead

Creek

(154)

LOYALSOCK

ROAD

STATE FOREST

Loyalsock

Trail

turn
left

WORLDS END ROAD

Run

stay
left

bridge

SPRINGS

bridge

Run

bridge

West

Branch

Double

Cottonwood
Falls

Double Run Nature Trail

Double

MINERAL

N

YOUR ADVENTURE

Adventurers, cross through the wooden arch to follow this babbling brook on the historical homeland of the Susquehannock. Cross your first bridge over Double Run and follow the green blazes up the trail. Turn right and follow the red blazes of the Loyalsock Trail and cross another footbridge. Soon, the green blazes of Double Run Nature Trail return on your left;

LENGTH

2-mile

loop

1,400

ELEV [FT]

1,000

Elevation
Gain

300ft.

DISTANCE [MI]   1   2   3   4

HIKE + EXPLORE 1.5 hours

DIFFICULTY Moderate—short, creekside romp with a small uphill at the end

SEASON Year-round. Can be snowy in winter (good for snowshoeing).

GET THERE The small parking lot is on the south side of the road just half a mile south of the state park visitor center on PA-154.

Google Maps: bit.ly/timberdoublerun

RESTROOM None

FEE None

TREAT YOURSELF Forksville General Store and Restaurant just up the road offers burgers and more for post-hike feasting.

Worlds End State Park,
Pennsylvania Department of Conservation and Natural Resources

(570) 924-3287 | Facebook @PADCNR

One of the smaller falls on the way to your destination

head that way and Cottonwood Falls will appear on your left. Power up here and take in the view. Turn left after the falls and cross another bridge, after which the trail heads uphill for a bit. Eventually you'll meet up again with that first junction with the Loyalsock Trail. Go straight on the green-blazed trail to return to the parking lot.

SCAVENGER HUNT

Solomon's seal

Keep an eye out in spring for these white flowers that hang like little bells. Gently shake the "bells" and take a whiff! Later in the season, red berries will appear. The large leaves appear year-round.

Polygonatum >

Gilled mushroom

Can you spot the gills on the underside of a mushroom? These gills are called lamellae and they produce spores that are dispersed by the wind to produce new mushrooms. If you find a mushroom at home you can see some spores by placing the cap on a piece of paper and covering it with a glass cup. Uncover it a few hours later and see what you find.

∧ This kind of agaric mushroom looks like an umbrella

Wild ginger

Check out these heart-shaped leaves carpeting the forest floor. Look even closer in spring—there are purple, three-tipped flowers hiding below! Wild ginger sits low on the ground so it can attract its pollinators, flies and gnats who are busy looking for food on the forest floor.

Asarum caudatum >

Jack-in-the-pulpit

This extremely cool flower has a green hood and red stripes. Where do you think it gets its name? Here's a hint: "Jack" refers to the green part sticking out of the middle (the spadix). Peer inside in late summer to see its bright berries!

Arisaema triphyllum >

Cottonwood Falls

You're hiking in Worlds End State Park. Does it feel like you've reached the end of the world when you get to this waterfall?

< How far is the drop?

34

FIND 18 FALLS AT RICKETTS GLEN

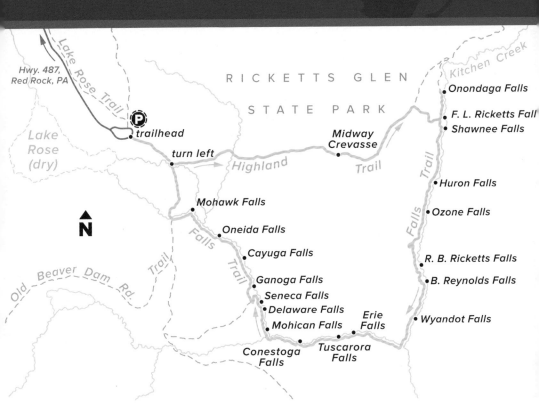

Hwy. 487,
Red Rock, PA

Lake Rose Trail

RICKETTS GLEN

STATE PARK

Kitchen Creek

Onondaga Falls

F. L. Ricketts Fall

Shawnee Falls

P trailhead

Lake Rose (dry)

turn left

Midway Crevasse

Highland Trail

Huron Falls

Falls Trail

Mohawk Falls

N

Oneida Falls

Ozone Falls

Cayuga Falls

Falls Trail

Old Beaver Dam Rd

Ganoga Falls

R. B. Ricketts Falls

B. Reynolds Falls

Seneca Falls

Delaware Falls

Mohican Falls

Erie Falls

Wyandot Falls

Conestoga Falls

Tuscarora Falls

YOUR ADVENTURE

You're hiking through a National Natural Landmark, a land of (at least) twenty-two waterfalls! Today, on the historical homeland of the Susquehannock, you'll pass eighteen. In 1868, Colonel R. Bruce Ricketts bought this land to get timber from it and built trails to the waterfalls. We'll start from the parking lot before quickly coming to a fork; for now we are going to head left on the Highland Trail. Step carefully through the roots and

LENGTH

3.3-mile

lollipop loop

Elevation Gain

715ft.

HIKE + EXPLORE 3 hours

DIFFICULTY Challenging—a bit long with a fair bit of elevation gain (worth it for all of these waterfalls!). Watch out for slippery leaves after a rain.

SEASON Closed in winter. Great foliage and high water in fall.

GET THERE From Red Rock on PA-118, go north on PA-487 for 3.7 miles and turn right into the park. Pass the Visitor Center and take the next right for the Lake Rose Trailhead parking.

Google Maps: bit.ly/timberricketts

RESTROOMS At parking lot

FEE None

TREAT YOURSELF Fritz Tastee Crème, just 20 minutes south on PA-487, has soft serve and a view of the Benton Dam to enjoy it by.

Ricketts Glen State Park,
Pennsylvania Department of Conservation and Natural Resources
(570) 477-5675 | Facebook @RickettsGlenSP

Get ready to see a lot of these!

rocks as you head downhill. Squeeze through the Midway Crevasse, take a power-up stop, and look for the trail sign—there is a shortcut to the two Ricketts Falls to the right or you can stay straight. We're going to go right; soon you'll see F. L. Ricketts Falls, our first of the day. Turn left here just to get a peek of Onondaga Falls, but then turn back to the trail you came from and keep going. You'll cross two wooden bridges and pass by five more waterfalls. At the next fork, turn right to complete the loop. You'll have to climb back up on the Falls Trail, but there are fun stairs the whole way. You'll see plenty more waterfalls before arriving at Ganoga Falls, the tallest of the bunch at 94 feet. Power up here and finish with Cayuga, Oneida, and Mohawk Falls. Reach the final fork you started at and turn left. High-five your partners eighteen times, one for each waterfall you saw today!

SCAVENGER HUNT

Wyandot Falls

Named after the Wyandot (also Wendat or Huron) people, this waterfall is wider than the others—do you prefer taller or wider waterfalls? Think about your answer throughout the day.

15 feet into a beautiful pool >

Maple samara

Grab one of these from the ground and toss it in the air to watch it helicopter to the ground. Have your hiking buddy grab one too so you can "race" them. Their shape allows them to be carried by the wind to make new trees elsewhere.

The fruit of a maple >

Ganoga Falls

How many steps can you count as Ganoga Falls heads downward? Kitchen Creek is a little over 10 miles long and is a tributary of 29.5-long Huntington Creek, which eventually connects to the mighty Susquehanna River (444 miles long!).

< Power up and enjoy the spray from 94 feet of falling water

Mohican Falls

You can *carefully* walk right alongside this waterfall on the stone steps. There are two drops here of about the same height—can you see both?

39 feet and right next to the stone trail >

Midway Crevasse

This rock is called Mississippian Burgoon Sandstone; it was created by sand carried in streams more than 330 million years ago. The sand was buried and turned into rock, and then erosion eventually exposed it. Touch the rock and give it a close look—what do you see?

< Walk through the crevasse (a narrow passageway)

35

BRING A HAMMER TO RINGING ROCKS

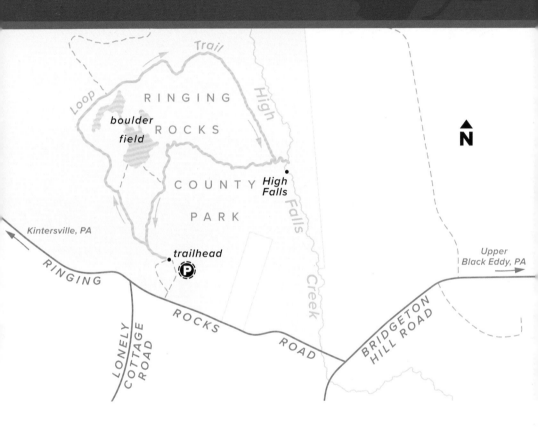

YOUR ADVENTURE

Adventurers, did you remember your hammer? You're on the historical homeland of the Lenape and about to enter one of the largest diabase (a special type of igneous rock) boulder fields in the eastern United States. From the parking lot, you'll quickly reach a fork and a trail sign. We'll head left for a clockwise loop. Start downhill; you'll soon see the boulder field on

LENGTH

1.3-mile loop

HIKE + EXPLORE 1 hour

DIFFICULTY Easy—short and mostly flat with plenty to see (and hear!)

SEASON Year-round

GET THERE From PA-611 / Easton Road in Kintnersville, take PA-32 / River Road east for 2 miles. Turn right on Narrows Hills Road for half a mile, then left on Ringing Rocks Road to find the parking lot on your left.

Google Maps: bit.ly/timberringingrocks

RESTROOMS At parking lot

FEE None

TREAT YOURSELF Chocolate in the Oven, across the river in Milford, has homemade candy, ice cream, cookies and more—perfect for grabbing a bag to enjoy on the trail.

Ringing Rocks County Park, Bucks County Parks and Recreation
(215) 757-0571
Facebook @BucksCountyParksandRec
Instagram @BucksCountyParks

∧ How many boulders can you ring?

your right. Take some time here to climb around the boulder field and gently hammer on the rocks to hear the special ring they make. Power up and keep going—there's more to see! Pass a stone wall and cross some planks. Keep going straight at the junction, after which you'll pass by a huge boulder and split rock. After you pass another couch-shaped boulder you'll soon see a trail to your left—hike up it a bit to reveal High Falls. Power up here then head back to the main trail and turn left. You'll see more boulder field access to your right—if you want to do some more ringing, this is your chance! When you hit the starting junction again, turn left to return to your car. Let the melody from the rocks ring in your head as you make your way home.

SCAVENGER HUNT

Tree burls

Look for these bulges in some trees. These bumps can be caused by insects, fungus, disease, or even something falling on or hitting the trunk. Sketch a burled tree in your nature journal.

How many "warts" can you find on one tree? >

Spotted salamander

Look for the bright yellow spots of this water-loving amphibian. They can grow up to 10 inches long and live for twenty years. How long is the one you found?

< *Ambystoma maculatum*

High Falls

This is the highest waterfall in Bucks County! The water flow can change greatly depending on the weather (that is, whether or not it has rained recently). What is the flow like on the day of your visit?

The 20-foot falls could be a torrent or a trickle >

Ringing rocks

This boulder field formed from molten rock that cooled quickly underground almost 200 million years ago. During the last ice age, ice and cold weathered the rocks, breaking them into these boulder-sized pieces. Not every boulder can make a tone; many of the boulders located around the edge of the field in shadier spots will make a dull thud when you hit them. You're most likely to find rocks in the center of the field that will produce the coveted ring (perhaps due to their density). Try a bunch and see how many bells you can find!

These are also known as sonorous rocks; which one makes the best sound? ∧

36

BOARDWALK YOUR WAY TO DINGMANS FALLS

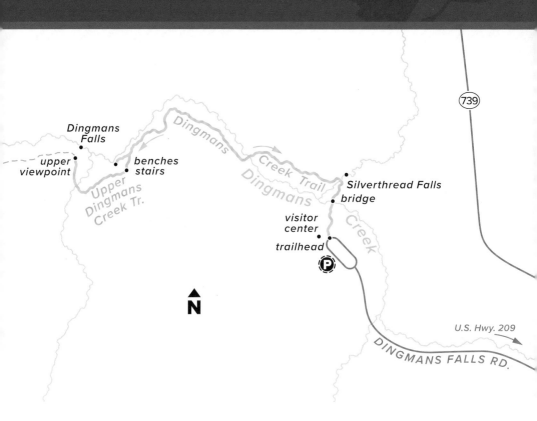

Dingmans Falls

upper viewpoint

benches
stairs

Upper Dingmans Creek Tr.

Dingmans Creek Trail

Dingmans

Silverthread Falls
bridge

visitor center

trailhead

739

Creek

U.S. Hwy. 209

DINGMANS FALLS RD.

N

YOUR ADVENTURE

Adventurers, today we'll be hiking on the historical homeland of the Lenape. Start your journey along the boardwalk and pass Silverthread Falls on the right. Keep an eye out for brook, brown, and rainbow trout swimming in the stream. Power up here, and continue on to reach Dingmans Falls, Pennsylvania's second highest at 130 feet! The falls and creek are named after

^ **Tumbling Dingmans Falls**

LENGTH

1.4 miles out and back

Elevation Gain
249ft.

HIKE + EXPLORE 1.5 hours

DIFFICULTY Easy—flat boardwalk to base of falls and stairs to the top viewing platform

SEASON Dingmans Falls Road closes in winter; some folks walk the 1.2 miles to see it in snow, but be sure to take necessary gear— the ice-covered waterfalls will reward your effort. Spring brings shade-loving wildflowers that carpet the forest floor. Busiest in summer.

GET THERE From Highway 209 in Dingmans Ferry, turn west onto Dingmans Falls Road and follow to the parking lot and Visitor's Center.

Google Maps: bit.ly/timberdingmans

RESTROOMS At parking lot

FEE None

TREAT YOURSELF Good Time Pizza (cash only), just 10 minutes north on Dingmans Turnpike, has NY-style pizza perfect for a reward after all the stairs to the falls.

Delaware Water Gap National Recreation Area
(570) 426-2452
Facebook @DelWaterGapNPS

Andrew Dingman, a Dutch settler who came here in 1732 and started a ferry service to get people across the Delaware River to New Jersey. Ready for one more challenge? Hike for just a little bit longer up the stairs for a view above the falls. After a power-up stop, go back the way you came and consider camping nearby at Dingmans Campground if you want to stay the night.

SCAVENGER HUNT

Sedimentary rock

As you climb the stairs for a view of the falls, try to take in the rest of the scene. The falls are surrounded by sedimentary rocks, which form from deposits of other rocks and materials. You might see sandstone and shale as ancient as 365 million years old!

View from the top of the staircase; how old do you think the rock around you is? >

Silverthread Falls

The perfect rectangles in the walls of this waterfall—the results of erosion—look almost intentional. How do you think the water could create these shapes? Can you see why it is called "silverthread?"

< 80 feet of beauty

Eastern hemlock

You're in a ravine full of hemlock—how much can you find? These evergreen conifers have needles arranged in a spiral that can sometimes look messy when you look at them closely. What do the needles look like to you? Look for its small cones on the trail. The hemlock wooly adelgid is an insect that loves to feed on these trees, which unfortunately damages them. Do the trees in the ravine look healthy to you?

< *Tsuga canadensis*

Great rhododendron

Look for these beautiful blooms in summer! The flowers are borne in clusters called "trusses" with spots inside that are a different color than the flower. Look at the color combinations of the rhododendrons here and try to re-create them at home with crayons or markers.

< *Rhododendron maximum* (*rhodo* means "rose," and *dendron* means "tree")

37

VISIT BUTTERMILK AND LUKE'S FALLS

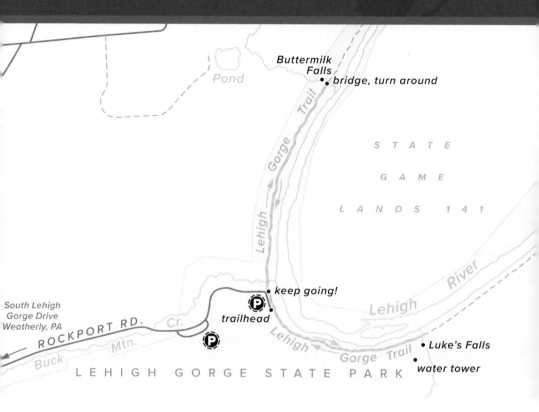

YOUR ADVENTURE

Adventurers, you're heading for not one, but two waterfalls on the historical homeland of the Lenape. From the parking lot, we're going to head left first on the Lehigh Gorge Trail, following the 109-mile-long Lehigh River, which begins at the Delaware River. Soon, you'll reach a small set of stairs; head down to reach your first power-up stop on a flat rock (be careful with

LENGTH

1.2 miles

out and back

Elevation Gain

105ft.

HIKE + EXPLORE 1 hour

DIFFICULTY Easy—short and flat; double the payoff with two waterfalls!

SEASON Year-round. Fall colors are spectacular.

GET THERE From Weatherly, head northeast on Main Street and continue on South Lehigh Gorge Drive, then make a slight right onto Rockport Road to reach the parking lot at the end.

Google Maps: bit.ly/timberbuttermilk

RESTROOMS At parking lot

FEE None

TREAT YOURSELF Dole whip, slushies, milkshakes, and more at Woods Ice Cream on Main Street in White Haven.

Lehigh Gorge State Park,
Pennsylvania Department of Conservation and Natural Resources
(272) 808-6192
Facebook @PADCNR

How do you think Buttermilk Falls got its name?

littles). Keep going until you reach Buttermilk Falls. Take your time here to observe your surroundings (maybe try sketching them in your nature journal) and then turn back the way you came. When you reach the parking lot, however, don't stop—we're going to keep going to see one more waterfall! After a short hike, stop and admire Luke's Falls (named after a former park ranger) and explore the nearby stone structure before returning to your car.

SCAVENGER HUNT

Dame's rocket

Look for these four-petaled flowers and make sure to smell them when you find one—the fragrance is beautiful. Unfortunately, this is an invasive species, meaning it can crowd out other native species of plants in the area.

What does this flower smell like to you? >

River rock

There's a lot of geologic history in this park; rocks as old as 375 million years have been deposited here by ancient streams. The rocks then folded 250 million years ago during a mountain-building event when the African and North American tectonic plates pushed up against each other. Take a piece of paper from your nature journal and fold it—what kind of force could make a rock do this?

< Relax on the rock

Water tower "castle"

Check out this old water tower, which was once used to help power the steam locomotives that passed through here. Take a walk around it and think about how it was constructed.

< Take a look inside!

Luke's Falls

Luke's Falls drops into the Lehigh River, which gets its water from 1,227 miles of tributaries and 256 lakes. It takes 24 hours for a drop of Lehigh River water to travel its 103-mile length! Float a leaf in here and imagine where it will go next.

< The beginning of a water journey

Mountain laurel

This shade-tolerant shrub produces tons of these gorgeous bowl-shaped flowers in late spring. When bees or other pollinators land on the flowers, their weight helps release the stamens inside the flower to fling pollen up into the air. Dip your fingers in some dirt then flick them in the air to fling your pollen.

< *Kalmia latifolia*

ADVENTURES IN
NEW JERSEY

Adventurers, we're about to embark on a journey throughout the Garden State, which attained statehood in 1787 becoming the third state. On the historical homeland of the Lenape, we'll travel from the very tip of this peninsular state, making our way from north to south to explore State Park, State Forest, National Park, Land Trust, Conservancy, and County Park lands. We'll begin in the state's plateau region, watching hawks on high at the state border between New York and New Jersey, head over to visit some forest fairy houses, and climb Pyramid Mountain and explore an old mansion. You'll cross boardwalks on the Appalachian Trail, find historic ruins along a babbling brook, and explore an old copper mine. You'll walk in the footsteps of history at Goat Hill Overlook and through the Princeton Battlefield on your way to a swinging bridge. We'll head to the Pine Barrens to explore a historic iron-making village and check out a bird-filled marsh and lighthouse. New Jersey's state motto is "Liberty and Prosperity"; feel grateful for both as you hike your way through this magnificent region.

38

STRADDLE THE BORDER AT PALISADES INTERSTATE PARK

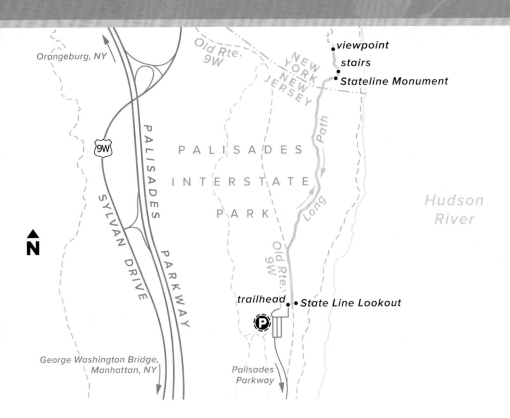

Orangeburg, NY

Old Rte. 9W

NEW YORK / NEW JERSEY

viewpoint

stairs

Stateline Monument

9W

PALISADES

Long Path

PALISADES INTERSTATE PARK

SYLVAN DRIVE

PARKWAY

Old Rte. 9W

Hudson River

N

trailhead • • State Line Lookout

P

George Washington Bridge, Manhattan, NY

Palisades Parkway

YOUR ADVENTURE

Adventurers, you are standing on an "exceptional resource value" wetland (in that it provides habitat for threatened or endangered species) and the historical homeland of the Lenape. Begin on Old Route 9W (a closed but paved road that was built in 1926) at the State Line Lookout. Soon you'll see the Long Path Trail (look for the aqua trail markers) start to the right; head

LENGTH

1.5 miles

out and back

600–

ELEV [FT]

200

Elevation Gain

112ft.

DISTANCE [MI]

1   2   3   4

HIKE + EXPLORE 1 hour

DIFFICULTY Moderate—short, but there are a few rocky steps and overlooks where younger ones need to be cautious. Watch for poison ivy year-round (don't wander off-trail).

SEASON Year-round. Hawk Watch in fall; only cross-country skiing in winter.

GET THERE Take Palisades Interstate Parkway to Closter and follow signs for State Line Lookout. Exit the highway and follow the road to the parking lot at the end (which can often fill early).

Google Maps: bit.ly/timberpalisades

RESTROOMS At parking lot

FEE None

TREAT YOURSELF Grab burgers, grilled cheese, or homemade baked goods from State Line Café right in the parking lot.

Palisades Interstate Park Commission
(201) 768-1360
Facebook @NJPalisades

Your goal: overlooking New York

that way to check out Balance Rock before the trail heads a bit downhill. Stay straight at the next junction and follow the rock steps to the Stateline Monument. You're standing in two states at once! Take care as you make your way through the gate and down the big stone stairs that follow. From here you can take in the views to the right, find the geomarker, and relax (safely, away from the edge) at High Gutter Point, a big rock outcropping. Look north to see the Tappan Zee Bridge and, to its left, Hook Mountain, the northernmost point on the Palisades along the Hudson. Turn around and carefully head back the way you came.

SCAVENGER HUNT

The Long Path

Set foot on the historic Long Path, a 358-mile trail that leads from a subway station in Manhattan all the way up into the Adirondacks. Hiker Vincent J. Schaefer first came up with the idea in 1931! How long would it take you to hike the whole thing?

< **Look for the aqua-colored trail markers**

Cooper's hawk

Named after William Cooper, who collected a specimen in 1828, this is a stealth hunter, meaning it likes to hide and pounce on its prey (often other birds!). Accipiter hawks have shorter wings to help them better navigate through the forest. Show your hiking buddy your best accipiter pounce!

Accipiter cooperii >

Stateline Monument

Surveyors, people whose job it is to mark land boundaries, used special new equipment to accurately measure and mark the state boundary in 1882. These granite markers were then placed at each mile to establish the new border. Today, markers like this one are rare; this is one of only two in the area.

< The Stateline Monument

Peregrine falcon

Join the Hawk Watch each September and October with other ornithologists (people who study birds) to look for this falcon. This cliff-dweller is the world's fastest bird—it loves to power-dive from up here down to the Hudson to find its dinner and can reach speeds of 200 miles per hour! Grab a pine cone off the ground and make it swoop down toward the ground as fast as you can.

< *Falco peregrinus*

Turkey vulture

Another subject of the Hawk Watch, this vulture forms a big V in the sky with its long, fingerlike feathers, which can help you distinguish it in the distance from an eagle or hawk. Turkey vultures can smell carrion (decaying flesh) with their big nostrils from very far away. Do your best turkey vulture impersonation.

Cathartes aura >

39

FLY THE FAIRY TRAIL AT SOUTH MOUNTAIN RESERVATION

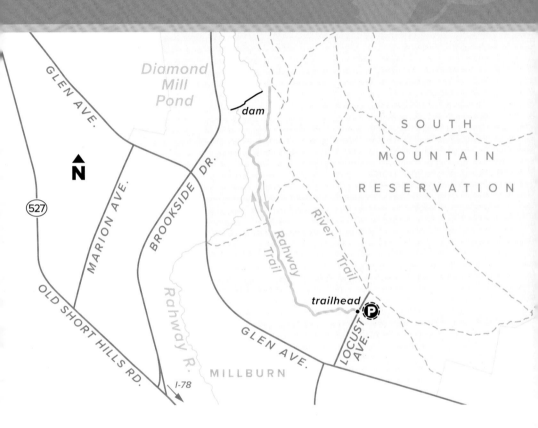

YOUR ADVENTURE

Adventurers, are you ready to enter the land of fairies on the historical homeland of the Lenape? Chief Fairy Officer Therese Ojibway began making these all-natural creations for fairies in 2016. The hike gives us a very good chance to practice our look-but-don't-touch skills! This amazing park trusts its visitors to carefully enjoy these magical creations without

LENGTH

1 mile

out and back

ELEV [FT]

400—

Elevation
Gain
35ft.

0

DISTANCE [MI]

1   2   3   4

HIKE + EXPLORE 1 hour

DIFFICULTY Easy—short, with so many
fairy houses to keep you occupied! Final
slope can be slippery so be careful with
younger ones. Watch for poison ivy.

SEASON Year-round

GET THERE From Main Street in Millburn,
head east on Millburn Ave, then turn left
onto Lackawanna Place. Turn right on
Glen Avenue and make an immediate left
into the parking lot. Free parking is also
available on weekends and holidays at
the Milburn Library on the other side of
Glen Avenue.

Google Maps: bit.ly/timberfairy

RESTROOMS At parking lot

FEE None

TREAT YOURSELF Spend a minute at
Splurge Bakery right down the street
deciding between their rainbow chocolate
chip cookies and Cake Buddies.

South Mountain Reservation,
South Mountain Conservancy
(844) 766-6266
Facebook @SouthMountainConservancy

So many nooks
and crannies to
explore with these
nature creations

damaging them. Therese visits weekly for maintenance and upkeep. For the first half-mile of the hike, as you follow the white blazes, count how many houses you find and compare your favorites with your hiking partner. Are you more drawn to those that look like traditional houses? Or maybe the mushroom gazebo is more your style? You'll soon reach Diamond Mill Pond and Dam. Take a leisurely power-up here and head back the way you came.

SCAVENGER HUNT

Fairy condo

The beauty of fairy houses is that they make magical use of their surroundings. Make some notes about your favorite fairy houses in your nature journal and then try and create your own when you get back home.

Imagine climbing the stairs to the fairy penthouse >

Big-tooth aspen

Look for the jiggy-jaggy teeth of these deciduous leaves (meaning they drop in fall). Feel the smooth white bark of the tree and find a fallen leaf to make a leaf rubbing in your nature journal.

< *Populus grandidentata*

Diamond Mill Pond

The 24-mile-long Rahway River (named after Rahwack, a Lenape chief) was dammed in five spots to provide energy for paper mills that used to operate along the river. Peer into the water to see how many different kinds of fish you can find. Several different species live in the pond.

Power up at this beautiful pond >

Eastern chipmunk

Look for this tiny striped mammal scouring the fairy forest floor for acorns, nuts, seeds, and mushrooms. Listen closely to hear its chip-chip or chattering as it munches.

< *Tamias striatus*

Fairy mansion

Find a small acorn on the ground and pretend it's a fairy. Make it fly around and explore (from a distance!) all parts of this complex creation built with an old stump as a base. How many fairy benches can you find? Stairs? Tables?

Whoa! >

40

FIND TRIPOD ROCK ON PYRAMID MOUNTAIN

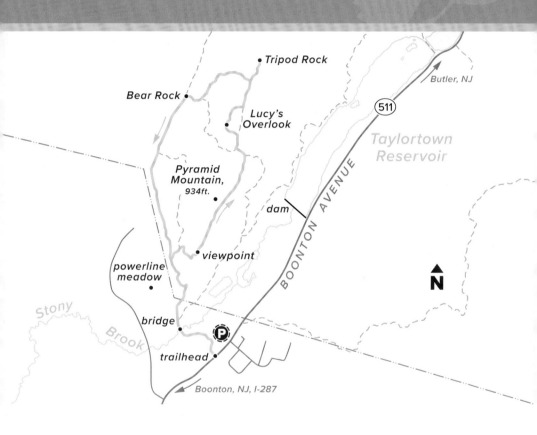

- Tripod Rock
- Bear Rock
- Lucy's Overlook
- Pyramid Mountain, 934ft.
- dam
- viewpoint
- powerline meadow
- bridge
- trailhead

511

Butler, NJ

Taylortown Reservoir

BOONTON AVENUE

Stony Brook

N

Boonton, NJ, I-287

YOUR ADVENTURE

Adventurers, are you ready to look for a precariously placed rock on the historical homeland of the Lenape? Begin your adventure by walking through the woods to a bridge over Stony Brook. Stay straight past the bridge as the path becomes a mowed strip and then passes between two boulders before heading back into the forest and uphill. Your lollipop begins at the next

LENGTH

3-mile

lollipop loop

ELEV [FT]

1,000 –

600 –

Elevation
Gain

296ft.

DISTANCE [MI]

HIKE + EXPLORE 3 hours

DIFFICULTY Challenging—one of our longer adventures with rocky and rooty terrain nearly the whole time

SEASON Year-round. Fall has migratory birds and beautiful foliage.

GET THERE Heading north from Boonton on Boonton Ave, find the large parking lot on the west side of the street across from Mars Park Corporate Center.

Google Maps: bit.ly/timbertripod

RESTROOMS None

FEE None

TREAT YOURSELF Curly's Ice Cream on Monroe Street in Boonton is a rite of passage for the neighborhood—grab yourself a homemade fresh berry scoop (or two) after your hard work.

Pyramid Mountain Natural Historic Area, Morris County Park Commission
(973) 326-7600
Facebook @MorrisParksNJ

Can you see all the way to New York City?

junction. Take the blue trail to the right and stay right as you go up and take another switchback. Power up here—the tough climbing is done! Take in the views of New York City from the ledge, then continue. Pass through a log gateway, turn left at the next junction, and then stay right on the blue trail. You'll come soon to a sign for Lucy's Overlook; turn left here toward the opening in the trees for another view, then continue on to reconnect with the blue trail. When you reach the sign for Tripod Rock, go straight to take in this geological marvel. On your way back, turn right at the Tripod Rock sign and step carefully downhill on the yellow trail until you reach the orange trail where you'll turn left and pass Bear Rock, the largest boulder in New Jersey. Continue straight on the orange trail to cross a series of planks over the bog and go through a boulder field (again, stay on orange). Pass some more plank bridges before returning to your first junction with the blue trail. Head downhill, back to the powerline meadow and your starting point.

SCAVENGER HUNT

Great mullein

Look for these rods in the open meadow under the powerline. The yellow flowers appear in summer, but you can feel their fuzzy leaves year-round.

Verbascum thapsus >

Oak gall

A gall wasp will lay eggs directly into the branch of an oak tree, and then this ball will grow out from the tree around the larvae. When the gall dries out, the baby wasps make their way through small holes out into the world.

See if you can find this fragile "cocoon" >

Tripod Rock

Deposited by the Wisconsin Glacier over 18,000 years ago, this large boulder is resting on three small rocks. Give it a push—will it budge? Grab some rocks and try to make your own tiny version of Tripod Rock.

180 tons balanced on three small rocks! >

Lucy's Overlook

Lucy Meyer was a conservation leader in the 1980s of the Committee to Save Pyramid Mountain; highways were being built nearby and this land was threatened by development. This great view and more are thanks to the passion and hard work of Lucy and other conservationists. Have you ever fought to save something?

< Make sure to take this side trail

Greenshield lichen

This leafy lichen might be visible on rocks or trees along the trail. Feel the small lobes and try to make your own acrostic poem for the word "lichen," where each letter stands for a word that describes it. L is for Leafy; I is for . . . Keep going!

< *Flavoparmelia caperata*

41

BECOME THE KING OR QUEEN OF VAN SLYKE CASTLE

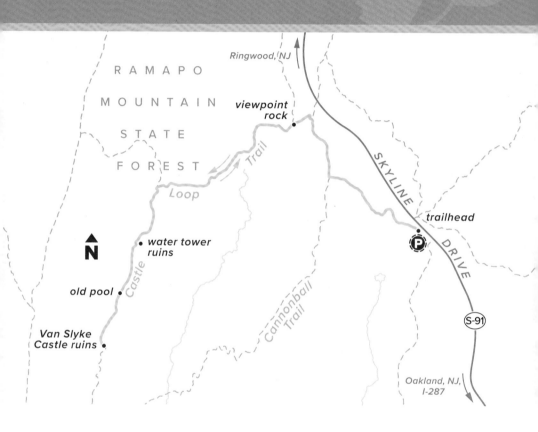

YOUR ADVENTURE

Adventurers, are you ready to be like Indiana Jones and find some ruins? Begin on the white-blazed Castle Loop Trail heading down into the forest—power up at the first big rock face. Turn right to come to a road, after which you'll turn right again very briefly and then turn left on the white-blazed trail on the other side. Follow the white blazes, stopping at a cool viewpoint,

LENGTH

2.2 miles

out and back

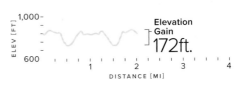

Elevation
Gain
172ft.

HIKE + EXPLORE 2 hours

DIFFICULTY Moderate—not too steep or long but a couple of rock scrambles and hand-holding spots for younger hikers. Bears are active so be bear-aware.

SEASON Year-round. Fall has great colors and spring rains fill the park's small streams. Parking can be difficult in winter.

GET THERE Take exit 57 on I-287 to Skyline Drive and head north for 1.5 miles. The parking lot will be on your left, and the trailhead is at its northern end. It can be busy on weekends.

Google Maps: bit.ly/timbervanslyke

RESTROOMS None

FEE None

TREAT YOURSELF Just a few minutes south, Oakland Bagel and Pastry is a great spot to snag egg-and-cheese bagels for lunch on the trail.

Ramapo Mountain State Forest, administered by Ringwood State Park (973) 962-7031
Facebook @RingwoodStatePark

Explore a twentieth-century castle!

and turn left onto a forest road for just a little bit, keeping your eyes peeled for a trail on the left marked with a wooden stake and a white blaze. Reenter the forest there. Head uphill for just a bit more until you reach the water tower. Keep going after that, cross between two logs, turn right, and find one more viewpoint. Keep a lookout for a foundation piece on the ground and eventually you'll come to the old pool. Beyond that, you'll reach the castle ruins. Carefully explore there for a bit and then head back the way you came.

SCAVENGER HUNT

Foxcroft / Van Slyke Castle

William Porter, a stockbroker, built this home in 1910 and named it Foxcroft (the location was then known as Fox Hill). After he passed away, his wife remarried into the Van Slyke family, giving the castle its current name. It was occupied until 1940, when it fell into ruin and was finally burned by vandals in 1959.

Former Foxcroft mansion on top of Fox Hill >

Water tower

Can you see the pipe connecting the water tower to the mansion? How much water do you think this water tower once held?

< How tall is the water tower?

Bull thistle

Look closely at the purple heads of this flower from spring to early fall—each contains hundreds of little florets! Bull thistle seeds are spread by the wind to help the plant reproduce. Bonus points: see if you can find a moth feeding on one of the flowers.

< *Cirsium vulgare*

Seasonal special: black raspberry

To find this berry in summer, look for these leaves of three. The plant is also known as black cap, because berries will pull off the branches hollow, like caps. Put one on each finger and wave your capped fingers at your hiking buddy.

< *Rubus occidentalis*

Pool

Behold the Van Slyke family pool. Draw a picture in your nature journal of what you think this pool might have looked like (along with the swimmers!) in the 1920s and 30s. How are pools different today?

 The old pool >

42

HANG OUT AT POCHUCK SUSPENSION BRIDGE

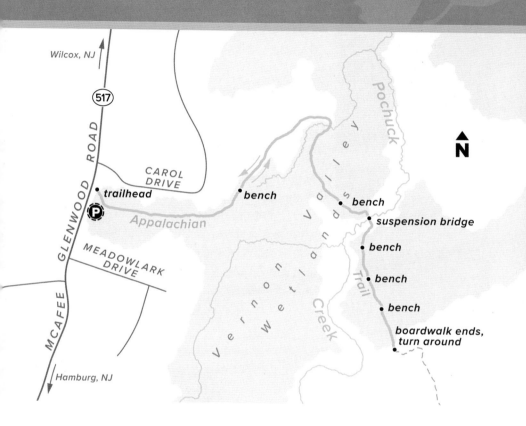

YOUR ADVENTURE

Adventurers, imagine the prehistoric lake sitting right below you on this boardwalk on the historical homeland of the Lenape (*pochuck* means "an out-of-the-way place"). This is yet another "exceptional resource value" wetland—think about how exceptional it is as you explore. You'll cross over 8-mile-long Pochuck Creek, a tributary of 88-mile Walkill River, which is

This boardwalk covers the swamp below—count the planks!

LENGTH

1.6 miles out and back

ELEV [FT]
600–
200–

Elevation Gain
29ft.

DISTANCE [MI]
1   2   3   4

HIKE + EXPLORE 1 hour

DIFFICULTY Easy—flat boardwalk most of the way; some shade spots, but can be hot in summer. Be bear-aware.

SEASON Year-round. Color in fall is spectacular.

GET THERE Take Highway 94 northeast from Hamburg and stay left to take McAfee Glenwood Road. Turn left onto County Road 517 North. In less than 2 miles, you'll see cars parked on either side of the road where the boardwalk crosses the highway.

Google Maps: bit.ly/timberpochuck

RESTROOMS None

FEE None

TREAT YOURSELF Holland American Bakery on NJ-23 in Sussex has homemade and imported goodies like stroopwafels and chocolate sprinkles you can add to anything.

New York-New Jersey Trail Conference
(201) 512-9348
Facebook @NYNJTC | Instagram @nynjtc

a tributary of the Hudson River (everything is connected). Head out on the boardwalk as it zigs and zags and have a seat at one of several benches along the way. There are many species of bird and wildlife to see here; with a little patience and a lot of luck you might just spy some. Continue for a brief stretch in the forest and then emerge to approach the suspension bridge. Keep going for another half mile until you reach the end of the boardwalk. One day, you might hike the more difficult Stairway to Heaven Trail up ahead, but this is plenty of adventure for now!

SCAVENGER HUNT

Suspension bridge
Beginning in 1995, this bridge and the 1.5-mile boardwalk took over seven years to build. The work was done by volunteers. Almost every board was brought in by hand. How many different boards do you think make up the boardwalk? Share your estimate with your hiking partner.

< 110 feet long!

Appalachian Trail blaze
Close your eyes and imagine you're hiking 2,190 miles over five to seven months, all the way from Georgia to Maine. What would it be like to camp every night? To see so many different states? To have to pick up food every few days and haul everything on your back? Do you think you could do it someday?

You're on a special trail >

American black bear

You're in bear country. There is no need to be scared, but there are a few important rules to remember: if you happen upon one, stand your ground, speak firmly and calmly to the bear, raise your arms to appear larger, and back away slowly (without looking the bear in the eyes)—*do not* run. It also helps to carry a whistle or make noise as you hike.

< Ursus americanus

White-tailed deer

As this mammal swishes its tail, look for the white fur underneath. You might see one poking and munching around and under the boardwalk. Stop and put your "deer ears" on—hold your hands cupped around your ears to make them big like a deer's. Can you hear more clearly now? Deer have big ears to help them better hear—and avoid—approaching predators.

Odocoileus virginianus >

Red-winged blackbird

Sit quietly on one of the benches and look for the bright red flashes of this blackbird's wings. See if you can watch one long enough to tell your hiking partner something special you noticed about its behavior. Does it fly high? Low? Fast? Slow?

Agelaius phoeniceus (agelaios means "belonging to a flock" in Greek) *>*

43

DIP IN THE TEACUP AT TILLMAN'S RAVINE

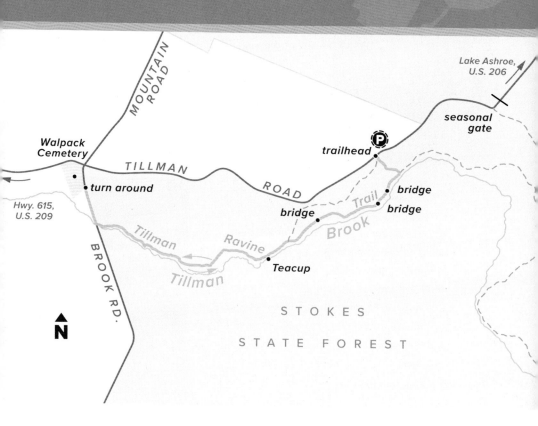

Lake Ashroe, U.S. 206

seasonal gate

trailhead

Walpack Cemetery

TILLMAN

turn around

Hwy. 615, U.S. 209

ROAD

bridge

bridge

bridge

Trail

Tillman

Ravine

Brook

BROOK RD.

Tillman

Teacup

Tillman

N

STOKES

STATE FOREST

YOUR ADVENTURE

Imagine being under thousands of feet of glacial ice—that's what this area looked like just 10,000 years ago. What will it look like in 10,000 more? We're hiking today on the historical homeland of the Lenape. From the parking lot, begin by heading downhill and following the white blazes on Kittatinny Mountain (1,803 feet tall). Pass a tree with maple tree signs

∧ **Watch Tillman Brook tumble into the Teacup**

LENGTH

1.6 miles out and back

Elevation Gain

368ft.

HIKE + EXPLORE 1 hour

DIFFICULTY Moderate—short but with a few steep parts

SEASON Year-round. Gate is closed in winter, which adds an extra mile each way.

GET THERE Take Route 206 south from Montague to turn right on Struble Road, which will turn into Dimon Road. Turn right on Tillman Road to find the parking lot on your left.

Google Maps: bit.ly/timbertillman

RESTROOMS At parking lot

FEE None

TREAT YOURSELF Try the breakfast sandwiches, fun cookies, and cannoli at Yellow Cottage Deli and Bakery just 15 minutes away on Highway 206.

Tillman Ravine Natural Area,
Stokes State Forest
(973) 948-3820
Facebook @StokesSF

on it and stay to the right. When you come to another fork, stay left toward the brook. Head down some stairs and try to limbo under a low tree. Cross a couple of bridges and pass a white blaze. Soon you'll reach a sign with the Teacup to the left and the cemetery to the right; head left and dip your toes in the small pond below the falls. This is a great power-up spot. Return to the trail and keep going toward the historic cemetery. Once you reach the cemetary parking lot and have a look around, head back the way you came. If you want to mix things up, you can take the upper pathway to the left; it travels above the ravine and meets back above the main trail. Consider spending the night nearby at one of several State Forest camping areas.

SCAVENGER HUNT

Crustose lichen

Look for this crusty lichen (fungi and algae living happily together in symbiosis) on rocks along the ravine. Wherever you see lichens, it usually means there is good air quality. Take a nice deep breath!

Once you know what to look for, you'll see lichen on so many rocks >

Walpack Cemetery

The former owners of this land, Nicolas Tillman and Lydia Dimon, are buried here in this nineteenth-century cemetery. Think about life back then as you read some of the names and dates on the headstones. Share some positive silent thoughts for these folks and their families.

< Pay your respects at the cemetery

The Teacup

The Teacup is formed out of eroded red shale and sandstone that is over 350 million years old. What do you notice about the rock that creates the Teacup? Dip your feet—or more—if you dare! This is a pothole formed by a whirlpool ("Walpack" means "whirlpool" in Lenape).

Take a power-up by "the whirlpool" >

Tillman Brook

What differentiates a ravine from a river? A ravine is created by erosion and carved into rock. Take a moment to listen to the loud babbling sound. See if you can hold a conversation with your hiking partner over the noise.

< **Listen closely to Tillman Brook**

Red-backed salamander

Put your hand on your lungs and take a deep breath. Now imagine you don't have lungs; how would you get oxygen? This amphibian breathes through its skin! Its coloring is sometimes red and sometimes black. In spring through fall, stop and look carefully in the leaves and by the rocks to see if you can spot one.

Plethodon cinereus ⌐

44

DISCOVER THE COPPER MINES AT PAHAQUARRY

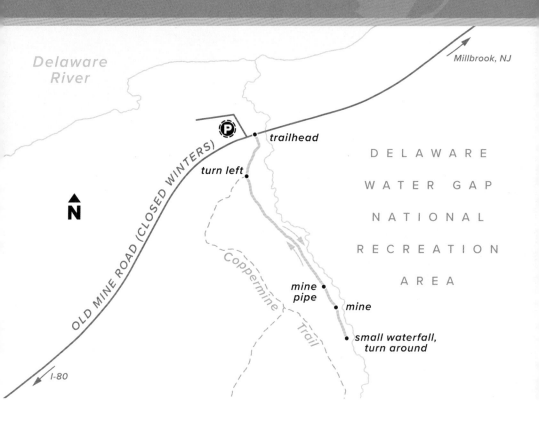

Delaware River

Millbrook, NJ

trailhead

turn left

OLD MINE ROAD (CLOSED WINTERS)

N

Coppermine Trail

DELAWARE WATER GAP NATIONAL RECREATION AREA

mine pipe

mine

small waterfall, turn around

I-80

YOUR ADVENTURE

Adventurers, the road you traveled on to get here is over 250 years old! You're on the historical homeland of the Lenape and what they call *Pahaquarra*, which means "the place between the mountains beside the waters." Begin at the Coppermine Trailhead. At the first junction, turn left and pass a stone wall and pipe, remnants of a former mining operation. The trail

LENGTH

0.5 miles out and back

Elevation Gain
98ft.

ELEV [FT]
600-
200-

1   2   3   4
DISTANCE [MI]

HIKE + EXPLORE 1 hour

DIFFICULTY Easy—short with a bit of elevation gain; be careful crossing logs to reach the mine and pool. Ticks and bears can be an issue in the area, so be bear-aware and check for ticks afterward.

SEASON Old Mine Road is closed in winter.

GET THERE From I-80, take the exit for River Road and drive north until it becomes Old Mine Road. In about 6.5 miles, the parking will be on your left near the river. Cross the street to reach the trailhead.

Google Maps: bit.ly/timberpahaquarry

RESTROOMS None

FEE None

TREAT YOURSELF Llama Ice Cream across the river in Stroudsburg has yummy artisanal scoops with exotic fruit for the bold and more familiar flavors for the less adventurous.

Delaware Water Gap National Recreation Area

(570) 426-2452

Facebook @DelWaterGapNPS

∧ Visit this small waterfall and pool after you see the mine

heads gently uphill as you pass a boulder and leaning tree. Keep a lookout for another mining pipe as you make your way. The mine will eventually appear on the right. What do you see when you look inside? Hike a bit farther to arrive at a small pool and waterfall. After a power-up, turn around and head back the way you came. Back at the junction, if you turn left, you'll eventually hit the Appalachian Trail, but for now let's head back to relax and reflect on the cool history we've just seen.

SCAVENGER HUNT

Mine adit

People have tried to mine for copper here since the 1750s, without much luck. The land was finally sold in 1918 to the Boy Scouts of America, who established Camp Pahaquarra, which ran until 1971. What kind of activities do you think they did here at camp?

< An adit is a horizontal opening that leads to a mine shaft

Pipe

Evidence of the old mining operation, like this pipe, can be seen along the way. Even though the mining efforts were never very successful, various groups gave it a go for over 100 years! Try and picture the old mine in action.

The remains of the mining operation are visible throughout the hike >

Stone wall

Can you locate any remaining structures from the old copper mill? This is where the ore removed from the mine would be processed to extract copper. What do you think the complete structure of the building would have looked like? Sketch it in your nature journal.

A mill once stood here >

Little brown bat

Little brown bats have used these copper mines sites in the past for winter hibernation. Sadly, the bats have been infected with white-nose syndrome, a fungal disease that is fatal for them and can spread to other cave-dwellers.

It is not known whether bats are still using the caves, so if you see one, send all your healing energy toward it!

< Myotis lucifugus

45

GO RUIN-HUNTING ALONG THE BLACK RIVER

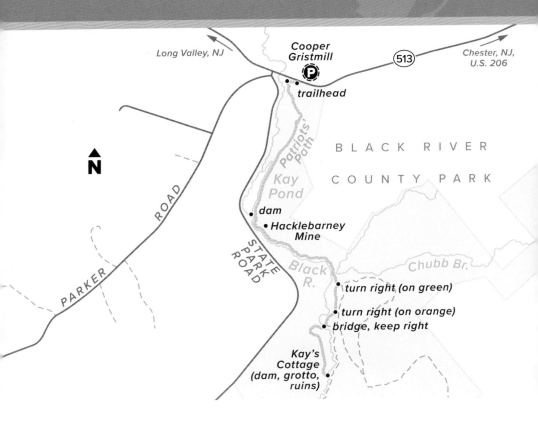

YOUR ADVENTURE

Adventurers, are you ready to go hunting for ruins? The goal of today's hike is to find Kay's Cottage and dam as you hike on the historical homeland of the Lenape along Patriots' Path. Take the trail from the parking lot to start off right behind the old gristmill and head down to the Black River. You'll cross a few boardwalks and puncheons (skinny, one-lane boardwalks that make it easier to cross muddy areas), all the while listening to the soothing

LENGTH

3.7 miles

out and back

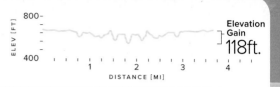

800–

ELEV [FT]

400–

Elevation Gain

118ft.

DISTANCE [MI]

1   2   3   4

HIKE + EXPLORE 2 hours

DIFFICULTY Moderate—fairly long hike with some rooty sections and a couple of gentle uphill climbs. Pay attention to the map at intersections.

SEASON Year-round, but closes a few days a year in fall and winter for deer hunting, so be sure to call ahead.

GET THERE From Highway 206 in Chester, turn left on West Main Street. The parking lot will be on your left in about a mile.

Google Maps: bit.ly/timberkays

RESTROOMS At parking lot

FEE None

TREAT YOURSELF Hacklebarney Farm Cider Mill, just a few minutes down State Park Road, offers cider donuts and other treats from their cool giant barn.

Cooper Gristmill and Elizabeth D. Kay Environmental Center,
Morris County Park Commission
(973) 326-7600
Facebook @MorrisParksNJ

Kay's Cottage in all its ruiny splendor

burble of the river to your right. When you reach a chain link fence on the left, look behind it to see the remains of the Hacklebarney Mine. Keep moving to pass a boulder, hill, and rock wall—and lots of ferns!—before reaching the pond's dam. Power up here and admire the rushing water. Continue on, passing an old driveway on your right. There are some great beach spots along the river, which offer great power-up opportunities. On the trail, stray straight again at a downed tree and cross more puncheons over a forest of skunk cabbage. You'll see the foundation of an old bridge at the next river pull out. Finally, you'll reach a junction; stay right here on the orange trail to drop back down to the river. Stay right again and cross the bridge, after which a slight uphill will bring you to the ruins and cobbled staircase leading down to the dam, grotto, and ruins. Power up here and head back the way you came.

SCAVENGER HUNT

Dam
What happens when you dam a river? What do you think this part of the river looked like before the dam? Besides swimming, what other reasons might there be for damming a river or stream?

The Kay family built this dam to create a swimming area >

Christmas fern
This fern has perfect little chubby finger leaflets! It gets its common name—Christmas—because it stays green all year long.

< *Polystichum acrostichoides*

Sugar maple

Has anyone ever said that you "furrow your brows" when you get angry? Sugar maple bark is furrowed, meaning it has deep lines in it. Trace your fingers through the lines and look for its beautiful red leaves in fall. In spring, look for its droopy flowers, which have little "rabbit ears" that collect pollen.

Acer saccharum >

Kay's Cottage

If you could build a summer house, where would it be? Elizabeth and Alfred Kay liked it here, so they dammed the river, named this "Hidden River Farm," and built this cottage. Imagine it with finished rooms, showers, a fireplace, and a terrace. Based on what you see here, sketch the finished cottage in your nature journal.

Knock, knock. Who's there? >

Cooper Gristmill

This is one of the last remaining water-powered mills in the state. The original gristmill was made in 1760 to help local families grind flour for cooking. Where does your flour come from?

This 1826 gristmill (built to replace the original) is where you begin your journey >

46

KEEP A WATCH AT GOAT HILL OVERLOOK

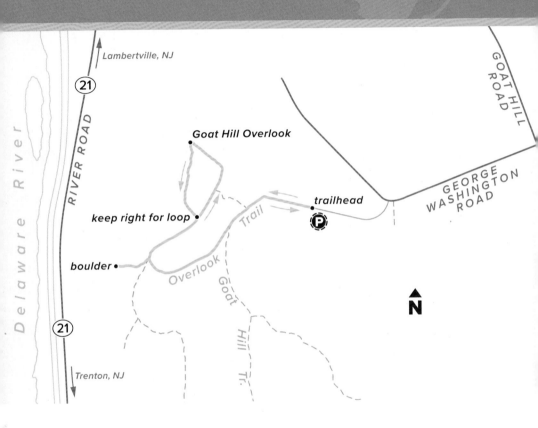

Lambertville, NJ

(21)

RIVER ROAD

Delaware River

Goat Hill Overlook

keep right for loop •

Trail

trailhead

(P)

boulder •

Overlook

Goat

Hill

Tr.

(21)

Trenton, NJ

GOAT HILL ROAD

GEORGE WASHINGTON ROAD

N

YOUR ADVENTURE

Adventurers, are you ready to grab an incredible—and important—view on the historical homeland of the Lenape? Start on the flat trail, ignoring most side trails and keep going straight. At another junction, continue straight. Follow the trail as it turns and power up on a large boulder to your left on a small side trail. Pass another trail to your left—you'll come back this way on the loop—and follow the trail to the right. Finally, reach the overlook. Power

LENGTH

1-mile

lollipop loop

ELEV [FT]

600–

200

Elevation
Gain
162ft.

1   2   3   4

DISTANCE [MI]

HIKE + EXPLORE 1 hour

DIFFICULTY Easy—short, wide trail with minimal elevation gain

SEASON Year-round. Fall offers amazing foliage, and the view improves even more in winter.

GET THERE Take Goat Hill Road south from Lambertville and turn right on George Washington Road. Stay left on the narrow access road to reach the parking lot. Note: the lot is small, but please don't park illegally. It's a short hike, so turnover is quick—if your family can be patient, a spot will open up.

Google Maps: bit.ly/timbergoathill

RESTROOMS None

FEE None

TREAT YOURSELF Snag a fresh waffle and a scoop at Nina's Waffles just across the river in New Hope.

Washington Crossing State Park,
New Jersey State Parks
(609) 737-0623
Facebook @WashingtonCrossingStatePark

Take in the view of the Delaware River and Pennsylvania

up and have some lunch here and imagine history unfolding as though you were George Washington. During the Revolutionary War, George Washington's army encamped on the PA side of Coryell's Ferry in December 1776. The Continental Army also crossed the Delaware here in June 1778 on their way from their Valley Forge encampment to the Battle of Monmouth. How many bridges can you see? How many towns? Look for New Hope, Pennsylvania, and the New Hope bridge. Continue on the trail through the woods with the river on your right-hand side instead of left, staying straight at both junctions then turning right to get back on the main trail. Head back the way you came.

SCAVENGER HUNT

Slimy salamander

Look for these amphibians crossing the trail in spring. They are black with orange or white flecks—like the night sky. They sometimes lay their eggs in stumps or in rocks.

< *Plethodon glutinosus* (*glutinosus* means "sticky" in Latin)

Lookout spot

Goat Hill Overlook may have been used by George Washington to keep an eye out during the Revolutionary War when his forces crossed the Delaware River on the way to the 1778 Battle of Monmouth. Imagine you're on a lookout now—do you see anything coming down the river?

< A view of New Hope, Pennsylvania, from the trail

Wineberry

These toothy leaves have pretty silvery-white undersides. White flowers will appear in late spring and berries will follow throughout summer. Consider making a "nature critter" out of any fallen leaves and berries you can find. What does it look like? Snap a picture to remember your creation, then put everything back where you found it.

< *Rubus phoenicolasius*

Smartweed

Look for the lance-shaped (long, pointed) leaves of this pink-flowering plant. Count how many flowers you can see sticking out when it blooms in summer.

< *Persicaria longiseta*

47

MAKE YOUR WAY TO THE SWINGING BRIDGE

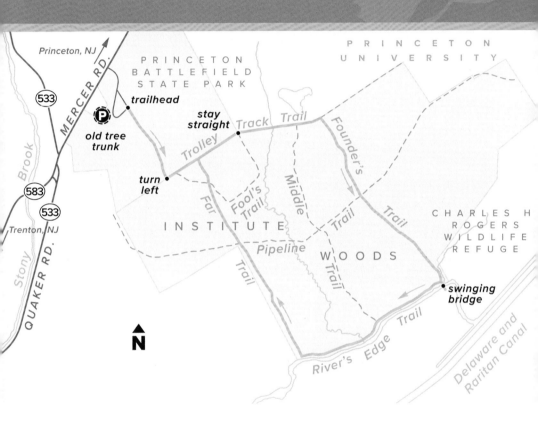

Princeton, NJ

MERCER RD.

533

PRINCETON BATTLEFIELD STATE PARK

trailhead

old tree trunk

stay straight

Track Trail

Trolley

PRINCETON UNIVERSITY

Founder's

turn left

583

533

Trenton, NJ

QUAKER RD.

Brook

Stony

INSTITUTE

Far

Fool's Trail

Middle

Trail

Trail

Trail

WOODS

Trail

Pipeline

CHARLES H ROGERS WILDLIFE REFUGE

swinging bridge

River's Edge Trail

Delaware and Raritan Canal

▲ N

YOUR ADVENTURE

Adventurers, are you ready to find a secret swinging bridge on the historical homeland of the Lenape? Begin by following the trail from the parking lot that heads toward the forest. Pass an old tree trunk and see if you can count its rings. When you reach a trail sign, continue straight to the meadow where the trail begins. You'll reach a junction; head left here. Stay straight at the next two junctions. Keep going past the trail marked "M" and finally

LENGTH

2.4-mile

lollipop loop

ELEV [FT]

400-

0

Elevation Gain

76ft.

1   2   3   4

DISTANCE [MI]

HIKE + EXPLORE 2 hours

DIFFICULTY Easy—flat and wide trail. It is a bit long so be sure to take plenty of power-up stops.

SEASON Year-round

GET THERE Take Mercer Road one mile south of Princeton University and turn at the sign for Princeton Battlefield State Park to find the parking lot.

Google Maps: bit.ly/timberswinging

RESTROOMS None

FEE None

TREAT YOURSELF You haven't lived until you've tried a Papa's Tomato Pie. Head south to Main Street Robbinsville to get yours.

Princeton Battlefield State Park; Institute Woods, Charles H. Rogers Wildlife Refuge (609) 921-0074, (609) 734-8000 Facebook @VisitPrinceton

How many planks are there all the way across?

reach the trail marked "F," for Founders. Turn right here. Keep going straight, following the F trail, and take a moment to admire the large trees towering above. Keep straight until you reach the swinging bridge. Be sure to peek around for frogs and enjoy the crossing over the 66-mile-long Delaware and Raritan Canal. This is a great power-up stop. Now, instead of going back the way you came, turn left from the bridge (on River's Edge Trail) to make a loop. Continue on, staying straight. Pass a tree cave and follow the trail as it curves to the right and stay straight past the junction with Pipeline Trail. You'll reach an intersection where you'll take a slight right. You'll soon reach a big tree and another junction; stay left here. After you reach the Washington monument, it's a straight shot back to the parking lot.

SCAVENGER HUNT

Jewelweed

This bright orange flower with red splotches is also called a "touch-me-not" because if you touch a seed pod, it bursts open. Don't worry though, it actually wants you to help spread its seeds. Give it a try! When it blooms in fall, look closely and see if you can find the seed pod hanging below the flower.

< *Impatiens capensis* (*impatiens* means "impatient" in Latin)

Beechnut

The American beech produces these fruits. If you find a burr like this one, see if the nut has already been removed by a squirrel or some other forager. Try to find as many as you can so that you can arrange them into a circle or fun shape. Take a picture of your creation so you can remember it later.

The fruit of *Fagus grandifolia* >

Green frog

As you approach the bridge, keep an eye on the water to see if you can spot this amphibian. It has two ridges along its back. If you see—or hear!—one, watch carefully to see how it jumps, and then see if you can jump the same way.

Lithobates clamitans (*clamitans* means "loud calling" in Latin) >

Gray treefrog

This one may be hard to spot—it is well camouflaged and likes to climb trees. Still, if you visit in summer during its breeding season, you might be able to find one by the water. Look closely at its warty skin and try drawing it in your nature journal.

Hyla versicolor >

Washington's monument

On 3 January 1777, Washington left behind 500 of his troop of 5,000 to keep campfires going so that the British Army would think they were still sleeping. Meanwhile, the rest of the troop marched 12 miles in the dark along the same trail you're standing on!

< **Look for this monument as you wrap up your hike**

48

FIND ALL THE BIRDS ON CATTUS ISLAND

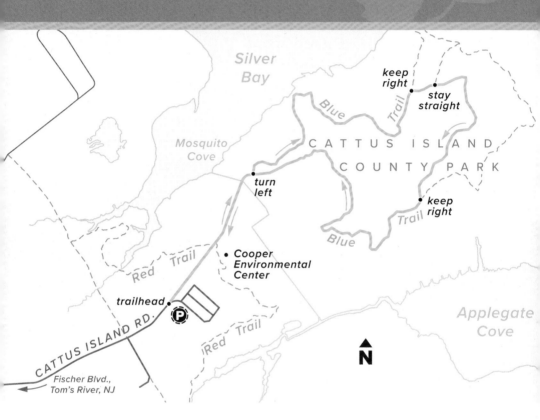

Silver Bay

keep right

stay straight

Blue Trail

Mosquito Cove

CATTUS ISLAND
COUNTY PARK

turn left

keep right

Blue Trail

Red Trail

Cooper Environmental Center

Blue Trail

trailhead

P

Applegate Cove

Red Trail

N

CATTUS ISLAND RD.

Fischer Blvd., Tom's River, NJ

YOUR ADVENTURE

Adventurers, time to explore this bird-filled wonderland on the historical homeland of the Lenape. You'll start out by going straight on a paved road until you reach the main (un-blazed) trail that passes the marsh. Stop at the first bench for a power-up and see how many different bird species you can spot in three minutes. Turn left on the Blue Trail, which curves through low

LENGTH

2.3-mile

lollipop loop

ELEV [FT]

400 —

0

Elevation
Gain

7ft.

1   2   3   4

DISTANCE [MI]

HIKE + EXPLORE 1.5 hours

DIFFICULTY Easy—flat and relatively short with nice even terrain

SEASON Year-round. From June to July, flies can be ruthless, so avoid early mornings and late afternoons or apply bug spray as needed (and check for ticks after your hike). Snowshoes recommended in winter.

GET THERE From Fischer Boulevard in Toms River, follow signs for Cattus Island County Park. Turn left onto Cattus Island Road for half a mile to find to the large parking lot on the right.

Google Maps: bit.ly/timbercattus

RESTROOMS At Cooper Environmental Center (check hours); portable toilets also available

FEE None

TREAT YOURSELF A few blocks south on Fischer Road, Mrs. Walker's Ice Cream Parlor serves homemade goodness. Which flavor will you try?

Cattus Island County Park,
Ocean County Parks and Recreation
(732) 270-6960
Facebook @OceanCountyParks

The view over the marsh

bushes—look for munching bunnies or deer!—around to a beautiful beach on Mosquito Cove. Power up here and look out at the houses out on Yellow Bay. Silver Bay, to the left, was the site of a Lenape encampment. Strike a pose on the rooty tree that landed on the beach. Keep going on the Blue Trail until you reach an intersection with a wide path heading to the left; stay straight for now as the trail narrows. Power up at another view of the marsh and find yourself back at the beginning of your loop. Turn left past the bench again and finish up on the same strip of land you started on. Don't forget to check out the Environmental Center when you're done.

SCAVENGER HUNT

Gray catbird

Listen up for this gray bird's song—it can last up to ten minutes and can mimic other birds' songs. If you hear it, try to do your own mimicking.

Dumetella carolinensis >

Great egret

Look for this majestic bird flying over the marsh, wading through it, or jabbing into it with its daggerlike beak while looking for fish. You can tell an egret from a crane by the S shape it makes with its neck. See if you can make your body look like an egret's.

< Ardea alba

Greenhead horse fly

Sometimes as many as seventy of these larvae can come out of one square yard of the marsh—they love it here. They also love biting *you*, so be careful in summer months. The bites aren't dangerous, but they are painful!

Tabanus nigrovittatus >

Osprey

See if you can find this bird of prey or its twiggy nest on platforms around the marsh. Osprey are also known as fish hawks—can you guess why? Stretch out your arms to get a feel for their large wingspan. They make an M shape when they fly—make your own M shape and see how high you can get!

Pandion haliaetus >

Lowbush blueberry

As you begin your hike, check out all the blueberry bushes around you. This plant will look different depending on the season. White flowers appear first in spring, followed by fruit, and then the leaves turn red in autumn and fall off, which means blueberry bushes are deciduous. Over winter, a blueberry bush gathers nutrients to get ready to perform the cycle all over again. Thanks for the show, blueberry bush!

Vaccinium angustifolium >

49

EXPLORE THE PAST AT BATSTO VILLAGE

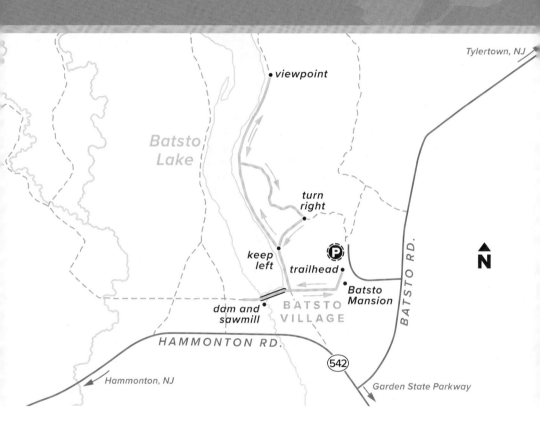

Tylertown, NJ

viewpoint

Batsto Lake

turn right

keep left

trailhead

Batsto Mansion

dam and sawmill

BATSTO VILLAGE

BATSTO RD.

N

HAMMONTON RD.

542

Hammonton, NJ

Garden State Parkway

YOUR ADVENTURE

Adventurers, are you ready to explore an old iron and glassmaking indus-
trial center on the historical homeland of the Lenape? The name Batsto
comes from the Swedish word *batsu*, which means "bathing place." From
the parking lot, head toward the mansion and turn right. You'll pass a bench
and reach the lake and a junction—go straight for now to quickly check out
the dam and old sawmill. Power up here for a moment, and then head back

LENGTH

1.5-mile

lollipop loop

Elevation Gain **32ft.**

ELEV [FT]

400-

0-

DISTANCE [MI]

1   2   3   4

HIKE + EXPLORE 1.5 hours

DIFFICULTY Easy

SEASON Year-round. The lake means flies in summer at morning and dusk, so plan accordingly.

GET THERE Take Hammonton Road east from Hammonton and turn left on Batsto Road. Take the first left to reach the visitor center.

Google Maps: bit.ly/timberbatsto

RESTROOMS At visitor center

FEE $5 for parking on weekends from Memorial Day to Labor Day

TREAT YOURSELF Royale Crown on South White Horse Pike is famous for their blueberry ice cream.

Batsto Village, Wharton State Forest
(609) 561-0024
Facebook @WhartonSF

The lookout over
Batsto Lake

to the junction and turn left to head uphill, with the lake to your left. Soon you'll reach another junction—turn left here onto the Blue/White Trail. After it narrows, you'll find a nice bench with a lake view before reaching another junction. Go straight here to continue to one more awesome lake viewpoint (if you reach the junction where the Blue and White Trails split, you've gone too far). Take a power-up and turn back the way you came. This time, turn left at that junction. You'll cross a bridge to an area where you can practice your plant ID skills with lots of signs to help. You'll soon meet up again with the Blue/White Trail. Turn right here and follow it back to the end of the lake. Turn left to return to the parking lot.

SCAVENGER HUNT

Mansion

Charles Read built Batsto Iron Works—along with this mansion—in 1766, which helped create items for the Continental Army in the Revolutionary War. Later, this was home to ironmasters William Richards, his son Jesse, and grandson Thomas. It was then purchased in 1876 by Joseph Wharton, a businessman from Philadelphia.

< The old Batsto Mansion

Sawmill

This water-powered sawmill was built in 1882 to make shingles and other lumber. Look at how the water of the 23-mile Batsto River, a tributary of the 51-mile Mullica River, rolls through here. How does the water power the mill?

The sawmill chugs away >

Pitch pine

Welcome to the Pine Barrens! They are called the barrens because early settlers could not grow their traditional crops in the dry, acidic soil which explains all the *low* shrubs around you. See if you can find any cones from a pitch pine. The tree drops them in fall and winter in the hope that birds and animals will open them up and spread the seeds. If you find any pine needles on the ground, count them—pitch pines have three needles per bundle (or fascicle).

< *Pinus rigida*

Atlantic white cedar

This tree loves wetlands and swamps and is an important resource for the Pine Barrens around you. Look for its pointy seed cones, which look almost like berries, in summer. Feel its scaled needles—do they feel different than the needles from the pitch pine? What do they smell like?

Chamaecyparis thyoides >

Cinnamon fern

Look for this wetland-loving fern on your hike. It can be tall with rounded leaflets (or pinnae). Look closely for the fertile frond protruding from the middle of the plant. It turns brown like cinnamon, which gives the plant its name. In fall, the plant can turn yellow.

< *Osmundastrum cinnamomeum*

50

HAWK WATCH AT CAPE MAY

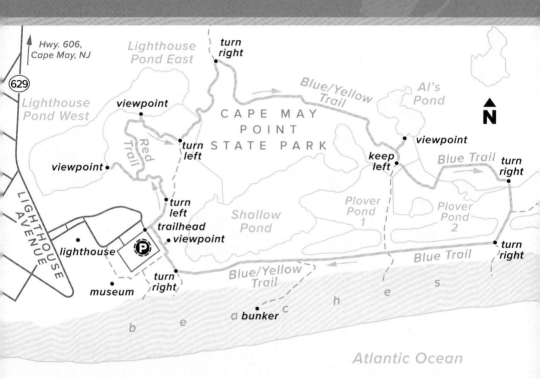

YOUR ADVENTURE

Adventurers, are you ready for a beach, boardwalk, and marsh birding
adventure on the historical homeland of the Lenape? Start on the Red Trail
by the Hawk Watch platform and stay left at the first junction. Take a brief
detour on the Yellow Trail for a view of the Lighthouse and Lighthouse
Pond West, then turn around and turn left to continue on the boardwalk.
You'll pass one more side trail to another viewpoint, this time of Lighthouse

LENGTH

1.9-mile

loop

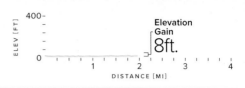

ELEV [FT]

400 —

0

Elevation Gain

8ft.

1 2 3 4

DISTANCE [MI]

HIKE + EXPLORE 1.5 hours

DIFFICULTY Moderate—flat, but walking on sand requires a bit more work (worth it for the views!)

SEASON Year-round. Flies can be very bothersome in June and July, especially in the morning and late afternoon. Fall is spectacular for hawk, butterfly, and dragonfly migration.

GET THERE From Sunset Boulevard on Cape May, turn left onto Lighthouse Boulevard. The large parking lot will be on your left.

Google Maps: bit.ly/timbercapemay

RESTROOMS At parking lot

FEE None

TREAT YOURSELF Just a couple miles to the east, near the beach, Fralinger's Salt Water Taffy is the perfect place to fill a bag with snacks.

Cape May Point State Park,
New Jersey State Parks
(609) 884-2159
Facebook @CapeMayPointStatePark

The still-operable Cape May Lighthouse was built in 1859; consider climbing it after your trek if you still have the energy!

Pond East. Power up here on the bench before continuing on the boardwalk. Take a left at the next junction on the Blue/Yellow Trail—we're going to head out to the marsh. You'll pass several more benches and then the boardwalk gives way to a dirt path. Continue until you reach the Yellow (only) Trail out to a viewpoint of Al's Pond. Return to the main trail and keep going until the next intersection, at which point you'll follow the Blue Trail to the left until you reach an opening for the beach. Take a long power-up here, watching the waves and looking for shorebirds. Return to the Blue Trail and head left this time, with the beach on your left and Plover Pond 2 on your right. This is prime bird territory! Stay straight at the next intersection to pass Plover Pond 1 and then Shallow Pond on your right. Take a look at the WWII bunker from 1942 on the sand to your left before returning to the parking lot.

SCAVENGER HUNT

Red-winged blackbird
Keep an eye out for the bright red shoulder of this otherwise entirely black bird. You might see it flying through the marsh, making a call that sounds like *conk-la-ree*! Give it a try—what does your call sound like?

< *Agelaius phoeniceus*

American oystercatcher
These black-and-white shorebirds like to hang out year-round at Cape May. In spring, they will dig shallow nests in the sand to lay eggs. See if you can spot one using its bright orange beak to crack open an oyster.

< *Haematopus palliatus*

Common whitetail

Cape May is all about migration, and dragon-flies and damselflies, as well as butterflies, will migrate here in fall. This dragonfly is a skimmer, meaning it likes to skim along the water. It has four wings and eyes close together (damselflies have eyes far apart). They prey on the biting flies that chase us around on the beach each summer.

< *Plathemis lydia*

American kestrel

People travel from far and wide to Cape May each fall to participate in the Hawk Watch. You can see over 36,000 different hawks migrate south to warmer weather! Create your own raptor (bird of prey) in your nature journal. You can draw it, build it, or write about it. Make sure it has talons, a sharp beak,

and good eyesight (the standard characteristics of a raptor), but get creative with the rest. What does your raptor eat? Where does it live? What special adaptations does it have?

Falco sparverius ⌐

Bald eagle

The bald eagle, the US national bird, is one of the many raptors that migrates through Cape May in fall. They love to fish with their huge talons. If you have binoculars, look closely for their stick nests, then try to build your own stick nest with twigs on the ground. What features make a good nest?

Haliaeetus leucocephalus >

ACKNOWLEDGMENTS

When you're in the world of everchanging trails and access, the tireless rangers, land managers, and stewards all worked hard to help me ensure accuracy of all our trails and species identifications. This book wouldn't be possible without the support of the following people: Blaise Simmons, Lisa Sideris, Elizabeth Shope, Mia Certic, Chris O'Sullivan, Matthew Shook, Josh Teeter, Fred Bonn, Michelle Johnson, William Hein, Rebecca Schultz, Rita Shaheen, Katie Palmer-House, Ryan Courtien, Alicia Sullivan, Henry Dedrick, Mark Simons, Peg Masters, Andrea Pedrick, Marissa Lathrop, Heidi Kortright, Armando Villa-Ignacio, Chuck Bartlett, Eileen Mowrey, Dennis Percher, Lori Laborde, Amy Lutsko, Eric Pain, Kristen Brandt, Susan Shutte, Jessica Kruegel, Rebecca Fitzgerald, National Park Service, Stancy Duhamel, Neal Ferrari, Audrey Wells, Stuart Reese, Elizabeth Shope, Barbara Wallace, Bill Hamilton, Chelsea Walker, Albert Wasilewski, Stacie Hall, John Laskos, Mary Rutkowski, Mitchell Stickle, Holly Hdzemyan, Al Tosi, Diane Folmar, William Kocher, Britt Smith, Scott Wilson, Erin McPeak, Angela Nagel, Diane Madl, Nicholas Sherlock, Arndt Schimmelmann, Maggie Enterrios, W. George Scarlett, Alan Delozier, Gregory C. Wyka, Carrie Seltzer, Matthew Pellegrine, Eric Nelson, Anthony Taranto, Chris Szeglin, and Brian Emelson. Thank you all for your contributions.

I also can't thank the Timber Press team enough for taking all of my photos, captions, and hike descriptions and turning them into the beautiful, functional book you are holding today. Thanks to Stacee Lawrence, Michael Dempsey, Julie Talbot, Melina Hughes, Kathryn Juergens, David Deis, Sarah Crumb, Sarah Milhollin, and Andrew Beckman for making this all possible!

And to my family—to Gail, Xavier, and Jaedon Moore for being my trusty guinea pigs, to my father, Alan, for being an amazing driver and hiker, to my husband, Garrison, for being head GPS tracker and cheerleader and chef, and to my mother, Ginny, for her research skills, impeccable parking, and uncanny ability to remind us it's time for more gas! This book is about family and having a strong family supporting you makes adventure possible.

And thank you to all of you for reading this and getting outside with each other! I can't wait to see the adventures you go on. Stay in touch at wendy@50hikeswithkids.com!

PHOTO AND ILLUSTRATION CREDITS

All photos are by the author except for the following:

INDEX

ABOUT YOUR LEAD ADVENTURER

Wendy holds a master's degree in learning technologies and is a former classroom teacher. As part of her quest to bring science education to life, she worked as a National Geographic Fellow in Australia researching Tasmanian devils, a PolarTREC teacher researcher in archaeology in Alaska, an Earthwatch teacher fellow in the Bahamas and New Orleans, and a GoNorth! teacher explorer studying climate change via dogsled in Finland, Norway, and Sweden. Today, she is a global education consultant who has traveled to more than fifty countries to design programs, build communities, and inspire other educators to do the same. She enjoys mountain biking, rock climbing, kayaking, backpacking, yoga, photography, traveling, writing, and hanging out with her family and nephews. Follow her on social media @50hikeswithkids and email wendy@50hikeswithkids.com.